BUMP AND RUN

It requires great determination and agility to go out in a strange city, find a willing and attractive sex partner, put her in a receptive mood, board her, and get back before the assistant coach looks in to see if your head is on your own pillow. This maneuver, in pro football circles, is now given the technical name of "Bump-and-Run." And just as bump-and-run has become a popular method of pass defense on the field, it has acquired permanent popularity on the motel circuit—not as a defense but . . . as a means of completing a pass.

BUMP AND RUN

The Days and Nights of a Rookie Quarterback

Marty Domres and Robert Smith

A NATIONAL GENERAL COMPANY

BUMP AND RUN:
THE DAYS AND NIGHTS OF A ROOKIE QUARTERBACK
A Bantam Book / published November 1971

Published simultaneously in the United States and Canada

Bantam Books are published by Bantam Books, Inc., a National
General company. Its trade-mark, consisting of the words "Bantam
Books" and the portrayal of a bantam, is registered in the United
States Patent Office and in other countries. Marca Registrada.
Bantam Books, Inc., 666 Fifth Avenue, New York, N.Y. 10019.

PRINTED IN THE UNITED STATES OF AMERICA

This book is dedicated, in gratitude and admiration, to the three men who, despite fearsome obstacles, turned me into a pro quarterback:

BUFF DONELLI
FRANK NAVARRO
SID GILMAN

Contents

1

The Dream World of Pro Football

What would have happened, I wonder, if I had not accepted the offer from Columbia but had gone instead to one of those football factories where you don't even have to know arithmetic? Would I have been any more resigned to spending my life as an ex-football jock? It could be.

It's too late to change now and I find myself a good part of the time fretting over finding a grown-up occupation when I am too old to play any more. This is not to say, by any means, that I don't like football. If I couldn't find a job playing football for money, I'd take a ball down to Central Park, New York, and play the damn game for nothing. But at least, if I had studied nothing but football after getting out of high school—the way a lot of mighty good men have done—I would not be the way I am now, chewing my ass out from time to time because I can't settle on a possible lifetime occupation that is of some use in the world. Instead I would be working at football day to day, anticipating only the thrill of steering my club downfield and making all my plays work—a thrill so heady that it is more to me sometimes than food and drink.

I would be contemplating a lazy, or at least a socially useless future in some square job like "public relations," whatever the hell that is, or peddling shares of stock to people who are impressed by my fame. And I would be able to sit down and write one more "sports" book that talked of nothing but football. Or of nothing but football and girls and good times. (I don't think you can have pro football without girls—and who would want to?)

1

But pro football is a sort of never-never land, as different from the real world as life among the very, very rich, or life in some Shangri-La where no chilly winds ever blow and where nobody ever grows old—or gets sick or goes to war or talks politics or notices that there are hungry people around. Even a black man in pro football has a hard time remembering what life is *really* like. Because inside this never-never land black men seem just like white men a good part of the time. They may have white roommates and are welcome at white men's parties and invite white men to theirs. They make the same money, generally, as a white player does, and they get just as much acclaim. And—at least on our club—there is no open prejudice.

It is a wonderful world to live in really, and sometimes you can half persuade yourself that the real world could be this way too if you could just straighten out a few hard-heads here and there. But the way my life has turned out, I am reminded all the time that while my football career lasts I am living in Limbo. I find myself stewing in my idle hours over such questions as the war in Viet Nam (it turns my stomach). Or smoking pot (I don't smoke it but I guarantee that some day it will be legalized.) or the National Guard, where I am engaged as I write this. (They put me on KP here for wearing a peace sign on my helmet.) Or the condition of black people. (Most of the blacks I know want to live in peace, like anybody else, but more and more of them have started to come around to the idea that violence is inevitable, the way the country is going.)

Would it be better if I had skipped the Ivy League education, then? Would I be a sounder citizen if I had become one of those guys with the whitewall haircuts that Florida's Governor Kirk and Spiro Agnew think make America beautiful? I honest to God don't think so. I think a man should be ashamed of patting himself on the back for being rich and successful and famous when there are men and women and small kids around who haven't enough to eat. And I think anybody who calls a country beautiful where black people can be humiliated and exploited just for being black has to be some sort of nut.

This discovery about myself—I mean the discovery that I had (fortunately or unfortunately) grown past the stage when I would prefer to be ignorant, as long as I was happy—came to me at a weird time. A bunch of us were visiting in Tijuana, where the big kick was the wide-open whore houses and where you are supposed to concentrate on getting laid in seventeen different ways and drinking cheap liquor and in general collecting a lot of wild "experience." But goddamn it, I had no eyes for the whores. All I could look at was those incredibly poor, wretched, *starving* big-eyed kids and the mothers, looking like ancient witches but probably only in their thirties. As we hurried on toward the whorehouses, I kept looking down the alleys where people lived worse than pigs do in Ohio. I kept asking myself why it should be this way and why some part of the world's wasted riches could not be put to work providing meals for those little boys and girls.

I went to the whorehouse district all right but I was damned if I would go in. With a couple of the other guys I waited around for the fellows who did go inside—and who came back in less than an hour to describe the dozen or more different ways the whores had demonstrated of doing what comes naturally to man and beast. I didn't believe a word they said.

As long as I'm making it clear how completely square I am, I should say that I really don't have much stomach for hired sex anyway. I used to wait on table in several different singles joints on New York's East Side, so I don't need any advanced study in the subject and I still like the whole business better when it's mutual. I even like girls better than football, if you want the truth. But I'd just as soon not find myself listed as a reliable "John" in the pay-as-you-go set.

During the playing season, sex in strange cities is usually taken on the wing, because of the brief time allowed between plane arrival and curfew. On this account, the ballplayers have adopted the term "bump and run"—the new pass defense cooked up in the American League—to describe the quick sampling of sex between arrival in the new city and bed-check. It takes careful planning, fast talking, and swift completion of the appointed tasks for a man to manage that schedule, especially in the Eastern cities where you lose three hours just flying through the time zones. Not even a traveling salesman or merchant sailor was ever up against the time problem that faces a visiting pro football player when he starts sniffing about for willing females in a new town. But you can get adjusted to it. Some guys even like it better this way, it being sort of a challenge. But more of that later.

Now that everybody is all clued in on my general attitude toward sex, sports, and segregation, I'll try to get on with the football part. This really began for me when I first flew to San Diego to meet the men I was going to work for. If you have ever gone to sign up, or even apply for a job, when your schooling was over, you can guess a good part of what was in my mind as the plane drew near the airport. Would I impress everybody as a leader? Would my voice be clear and confident? Would my handshake be firm enough? Would I talk too much, or too little? Would they think my hair was too long or my clothes too square?

I had rehearsed in my mind the first meeting with the emissary from the San Diego Chargers. I don't recall now just what sort of guy I had pictured. Probably some football type, in my own range of size (I am six-four and weigh 215). Or perhaps some sleek millionaire, or a John Wayne type of coach. What I found really shook me for a second or two. It was a guy who might have been got up as a comic Californian—shorts, wild shirt, and a pair of those headlight-size sunglasses on a man not much wider than a fish pole. This was a football player? Or was it just California?

As it turned out, the man, Bob Hood, was one of the friendliest and best-met men I ever ran into. Just what his title was supposed to be I forget, but his work was as a general trouble-shooter and dry-nurse for the rookies. His immediate job with me had been to arrange for my enlistment in the National Guard and to fill me in on all the details of my commitment. I felt no pressure to overwhelm him with my leadership qualities. He was just a real nice guy who was glad to see me and made me feel sincerely welcome. He even made it seem a bit easier to go ahead now and meet the bosses.

I met the bosses in the office. As never fails in such meetings, the names and faces got a little mixed up. But I sure as hell knew Coach Gilman,* a man who seemed to buzz with inner energy—very outgoing, without a trace of affectation. I shook his hand firmly and returned his welcome in a good clear voice (leadership! leadership!). Everybody loaded me with cordiality. (My lawyer had not signed the deal yet!) And I was so concerned with the impression that I was creating, and fretting so much over what *I* would say next that I hardly retained a drop of all the wisdom that was poured out on me at that first meeting.

My next big concern was meeting John Hadl, the Charger first-string quarterback and the man who, one might have supposed, would be my natural enemy on the squad—the man whose job I hoped to take some day. My meeting with John was also under rather unexpected circumstances. Because, for God's sake, I met him between periods of a boys vs. girls basketball game!

This was pro football players against a team of airline hostesses. The game was a lot of laughs—but John looked like an athlete on the court. You can always tell by the way a man moves about, sure-footed, slick, and fast. But he made the greatest impression on me between the halves, sitting down, calmly inhaling a beer and chugging on a big cigar. I don't know if it was the cigar or just his general air of composed self-confidence that got me. Real *real* cool! I thought. How could he be cooler? My admira-

---

* During the 1970 season, Sid Gilman turned over the coaching job to Charley Waller, who had been his assistant, and Sid took himself upstairs, as general manager and as chief observer from the press box. Sid did this for health reasons. Whether he felt better or worse at the end of the season I don't know, but now he is back as coach and Charley is once more Sid's assistant.

tion for John began right at that instant and it has never diminished.

John greeted me without the least uneasiness and all the qualms I had had about the meeting quickly dissolved. This guy, I decided, was going to be a friend of mine if I could manage it, and it didn't matter at all if we were after the same job. There had to be room for the two of us anyway and the Chargers would wind up, I told myself (being full of confidence by now at the way the meetings had gone), with *two* first-string quarterbacks.

Workouts in the beginning were just with the other rookies and hardly provided any test at all—either of how I was going to make it in pro football or how I would be received by my teammates. (I knew I had to expect some resentment from the veterans who would be loyal to John.) It was not until we began to work out with the veterans that I had my first real letdown. It was a silly damn thing but at the time, when I was taking everything so seriously and giving myself the "leadership! leadership! confidence! confidence!" routine, it handed me a small jolt.

I was throwing passes to Lance Alworth, who is the best pass-receiver in the business, the surest-handed, the most confident, the craftiest. I let go a long one to Lance. It may have had a bit of a wobble to it (some of my passes did in the first days) but it reached Lance right in stride. He took it in his fingers and snuggled it away. I drew in a deep breath that tasted as sweet to me as sugar water, I was so pleased with myself. Lance trotted back to me and I got set to play the part of the Modest Leader brushing off a compliment. But there was no compliment. With that little giggle that I soon learned preceded just about every remark Lance made, he told me: "John gives them to me right *here*." He indicated a spot in the hollow of his shoulder.

A month or so later, if Lance had made any such remark to me I most likely would have told him to go screw himself. But at that point in my career this mild criticism, when I had expected a slap on the back, really bit into my soul.

Sitting here now in my National Guard green fatigues and looking back to that moment, I marvel at all the growing up I have done in a spring, summer, and fall. In so many ways. In my attitude toward my teammates, in my attitude toward football, in my attitude toward the world. There was a time not so long ago when I was perfectly ready to envision the same sort of future a lot of guys—a lot of perfectly decent guys, good companions, broad-minded, generous—look forward to: an executive or coaching job in football, or a nice tame occupation like advertising. Plenty of men get into jobs like that and seem to have a hell of a good time out of life. But already I feel I am disqualified for any such future.

I am unable for one thing to listen to all the gung-ho "killer" routine around me without giving a silent cheer for the Peace Corps. (My outfit even has a college-type cheer, something like: "B-6! Killers all! Yea, Army!") Our C.O. assured us at the start that he was going to turn us all into "professional killers." Not me, I promised myself. I am no pacifist. But I am goddamned if I am going to allow someone to persuade me that there is any *fun* in killing. One of my best friends is a draft-dodger (his father disowned him, for God's sake). And while I would never follow his path, I find it a hell of a lot easier to sympathize with him than I do with some of these Permanent Party creeps who are as gung-ho about battle as sane school kids are about football. They *brag* of shooting prisoners and of carrying strings of dried *ears,* for Christ's sake, cut off Viet Cong bodies. Is this civilization?

Of course I realize that there is a measurable amount of bullshit in the stories these regular army guys deal in. But even so, what kind of guy is it who thinks he is making points for himself by bragging about shooting helpless people or mutilating dead bodies or piling up corpses to provide a "body count"? Yet these are among the "America the Beautiful" people that Spiro Agnew thinks are worth ten times as much as the kids who refuse to travel ten thousand miles to murder some strangers.

Well, back to pro football. There is an immediate difference between pro football and college football. The professional attitude won't admit of any of that die-for-dear-old-Rutgers crap, on the part of either the coaches or the players. A pro locker room never gets charged up with the hope of a glorious victory over some ancient rival. And no pro coach who was not a certified nut would go in for the phony dramatics you often see in a college locker room. Some college coaches will even set up a whole stack of furniture or piece a broken blackboard together just so they can knock it over, or smash it into pieces with one blow at the climax of a "fight" speech. I can picture some of our hard-bitten veterans watching a performance like that. They wouldn't laugh. They'd probably puke.

But there is plenty of spirit, just the same. I can't imagine anybody being more gung-ho about the game than Coach Gilman. And I never had the good fortune to play on a college club where there was any more desire than there was on the Chargers when we seemed to have a chance for the play-offs. These guys wanted to *win*. They wanted to make good on their jobs. They hungered after that top prize and they were ready to pulverize the clubs that tried to stop them. They would fight like wolves to help a teammate, particularly a man like John Hadl, to whom the whole club is devoted.

Players are impressed by a coach who works hard and plays fair. When they are sweating their balls off on the field they want to see the coaches out there too, making note of their efforts and giving them credit for what they accomplish. One method a lot of pro coaches go in for (and a method I personally deplore) is the free use of sarcasm. Somehow they think it juices a guy up if they needle him good and hard during practice. But I know many players violently resent it. Some resent it not for their own sake but for the sake of a hard-working veteran who is pouring out blood and sweat as freely as he can manufacture them.

We have one coach who makes a specialty of nagging one of the veteran guards—a player who tries as hard as any man in the squad and a good deal harder than the man ahead of him (who has more speed and natural skills). The player doesn't need this type of public ridicule to make him try. These constant suggestions that (after six seasons) he is about to be cut just pull the guy down. Some of the men on the squad feel that the coach is discharging some of his own hostility on the player.

What a pro football player expects of a coach is some personal respect, as long as he is putting out full effort. A good coach is a guy who makes allowances for a man's shortcomings, who gives a guy credit for effort, and who bears down only on mental lapses and lack of hustle. Hustle! That's what makes for a good practice, for confidence, for team loyalty. In a good squad *everybody* hustles.

We had plenty of hustle in rookie camp and lots of confidence too. I found myself thinking that Coach Gilman himself was too free with the sarcasm sometimes, forgetting he was dealing with grown men. But that's his way and nobody could say that he failed to set an example of hustle. Working with the rookies before the veterans came to camp, he was full of good advice, full of praise, full of good spirits. We had a little guy named Mike Simpson, from Houston, who was only five-feet-six, about as small a man as I've ever seen on a pro football team. But he could do a hundred yards in 9.5 seconds and he *worked*. And Coach Gilman put in a lot of time with Mike, trying to turn him from a defensive back into a wide receiver, building his confidence, patiently correcting his mistakes. It really was a thrill to see this great little guy respond to the coach's build-up. And yet, underneath all his show of confidence and his grim effort, you began to sense that Mike *knew* somehow he was not going to make it. His confidence was all on the surface, more of a fierce hope, I guess, than a real conviction. He had been a fifteenth-round draft choice and had come to camp telling himself he was a long shot.

I used to read and hear about the suddenness of the
blow that comes when a guy is cut from the squad—the
shock of the news, the effort to rearrange your shattered
world. But this is not the way it happens. When the blow
is coming, the guy knows it and knows it well. He may not
be resigned to it, may resent it bitterly and tell himself
he'll come back some way and show the coach he has
made a mistake. But still he sees the cut coming far in
advance.

Little Mike Simpson saw it. As soon as Lance Alworth
and Gary Garrison came to camp, the coach had less
and less time for Mike. And Mike's morale began to
droop. Evenings, instead of playing his guitar and belting
out the country music he loved and we loved to listen to,
Mike would talk about being cut and going home to his
wife. But of course he kept trying, trying too hard. He
pressed in practice and in pre-season games. Then he
fumbled a punt and he knew the struggle was over. They
kept him around another week but hardly noticed he was
there. The final day he went around to every member of
the squad and wished each man well. There was not a
guy in the room that did not wish Mike could have stayed.
I could see the tears in his eyes. He'd known it all the
time. And yet he had clung to that wild hope!

It was different with Craig Cotton, my rookie rommate
and my good friend. Craig, like all our black players, was
full of pride. He knew what it meant too when the coaches
started giving him less and less attention. It was something
like being sized up for a fraternity. You *know*, despite the
politeness and the jollity, that you have been marked lousy.
But Craig was not taken down a damn bit, he was just
mad. If they cut him, by God, they were wrong! And he
would catch on somewhere else and make them wish they
hadn't. I'll have to tell you about Craig, because he was
something else.

Craig was a dark-brown guy, not really black. But he
called himself black. Lots of gray-faced guys call themselves white, so I see nothing wrong with that.

Craig was not especially political. He knew and re-
spected the black leaders. But for himself, he was inter-

ested in football and in girls. These were two enthusiasms
we shared, and so we made perfect roommates.

Craig and I came to know each other quickly because,
being together at the spring "preview" for rookies, we
shared, along with three other guys, the same Ford station
wagon when we set out to tour San Diego in search of
beer and broads. Then, when we roomed together at
rookie camp in Irvine, we became close friends. When Sid
Gilman first saw Craig—who was six-feet-four and weighed
just a bucketful more than 200 pounds—he told him to
put some weight on. Craig, a tight end, was in no shape to
take on a defensive end who might have an edge of fifty
or sixty pounds. So Craig reported to our "strength coach,"
Maylen. ("He knows a lotta shit about weights, maaaan!"
Craig explained to me.) At regular camp, after a regimen
of five meals a day, plus protein milkshakes and lots of
weight-lifting, Craig punched in at 230, ready to take on
Deacon Jones or any other like him.

Craig really had a tough assignment with the Chargers.
Ahead of him were two veterans—Jacque MacKinnon and
Willie Frazier—each of whom stood about two inches
taller than Craig and outweighed him by at least 15
pounds. But never in my life have I seen a more ambitious
football player than Craig. He was a fanatic! He *knew* he
could make the grade and he didn't care who was ahead
of him.

But don't think for a minute that Craig was one of
these "eat-sleep-and-breathe-football" types, the kind that
can drive you up a wall and turn you against the whole
game. Craig was a perfectly normal rookie—that is, he
spent most of his off-gridiron time sniffing out the relatively
few females who roamed the big Irvine campus. Before
we had been there a week, you could not walk past one
girl, in Craig's company, and not have him hail her by
name. No question about it, if they were to select an All-
Pro in this department, in which every player on every
club is a potential star, Craig would get every vote. And,
by training camp rules, you could not even shift your
weight in a girl's direction if any member of the coaching
staff was within a hundred yards.

Craig was efficient in this field nonetheless. He never missed a curfew. As a matter of fact he almost always beat the bell by twenty or thirty minutes. And before he hit the sack, he would pore over that play book one more time or two. He "studied" every night, no matter what else he did first.

Craig's devotion paid off in performance. There wasn't a player on the field who put out the way Craig did—in calisthenics, in blocking drill, in pass catching. Sid Gilman simply could not keep his eyes off him and was forever walking up to deal him a congratulatory whack. He would patiently explain some move to Craig, and Craig would hop into the drill and execute perfectly, to Sid's loud acclaim. Or Craig would reach up out of a crowd of defenders and snag a pass with his fingernails and Sid would turn to anyone who stood by and exclaim: "Some day he's going to be a *great* one, that young one is!"

This sort of meat would cause some guys to begin to strut a little. It might even make them dodge the hard parts of the drill and save themselves for the big moments when there was a pass to catch or a dazzling move to make. Not Craig. The more Sid praised him, the more Craig would work his ass off. In every way Craig was the sort of guy that football coaches must dream they are going to come up with in the draft.

There was never any feeling, on Craig's part, that he was being exploited or taken advantage of, or put down in any way. He loved his job and *knew* that he was going to make good at it, and land in the big money. Not that he really hungered after money, the way some guys might who had come out of a ghetto background. Craig had always lived well. He pushed an Eldorado of his own—which his loving mother, for God's sake, had driven all the way from Pittsburgh so Craig could have it in camp. As for threads, Craig was All-Pro there. Pro football players are all more than a little clothes happy. But Craig lit up the landscape when he set sail. His suits were tailor-made—flare bottom pants, shaped jackets—and his shirts would dazzle a snake. He had a case full of neckties, all

wild enough to serve as backdrop for a psychedelic med-
icine dance, and he had over-the-calf boots that gleamed
like the radiator of a new Rolls Royce.

When Craig and I stepped out together—which was
every night when he had not already lined up some sum-
mer-school honey—I felt like the poor relation, for I was
still Ivy-league conservative, even in the best threads I
owned. During my years at Columbia, California styles had
not yet made many converts on the campus. Craig not
only outshone me in the wardrobe division, he was a
champion at heavy rapping—i.e., bullshitting—and would
pitch into any subject, in any company, and soon take
over. He was not a guy given to brooding and was the
best companion of any guy I ever played ball with, always
ready for any sort of action, always ready to laugh, always
agreeable.

When the vets came to camp, Craig was at his peak—
in his performance and in his optimism. Whoever these
guys were who stood ahead of him, they were not going
to keep Craig Cotton off the first string. But Sid Gilman
obviously thought different. With Frazier and MacKinnon
on hand, Sid had less and less time for Craig and it
gradually became obvious that Craig was not going to
play tight end for San Diego that season.

Another guy would have begun to mope a little, or
have put on a face of phony cheer. But not Craig Cotton.
He was hot! If he was not going to be the Chargers'
tight end, then he'd play tight end for some other club!
One way or another, he used to assure me, you'll be hearing about Craig Cotton.

Gilman apparently wanted to slip Craig on the taxi
squad without having some other club pick him up on
waivers. So he kept him out of action, except for appearances on the specialty squads—kickoff and kick
return. But Craig was a hard-nosed boy when it came to
business dealings. In that way I think he must have taken
after his mother, a wonderful-looking, willowy lady who
could have been taken for thirty and was really fifty.

Craig was very proud of his Mom. One day I was goofing off in our room when I heard Craig's loud bellow downstairs:

"Marty! You get your ass down here in a hurry! Move!"

My conscience being always ready to jump to life when I was flaking out somewhere, I leaped right to my feet and grabbed at my notebook. My God! Had I forgotten a meeting again? I plunged for the door ready to make the stairs in three jumps. But on the landing I almost bowled right into a tall black lady who was standing at Craig's side.

"Marty!" said Craig, and he was near bursting with pride, "This is my MOM!"

Well, Jesus, I thought, why shouldn't he be proud? This tall, regal, gentle-looking lady who could have been an older sister! Mrs. Cotton practically took me into the family with her smile. Craig, she said, had told her *all* about me. With that, she gathered me right into the group and we went outside to have one of the other rookies take pictures of us together.

But what I was saying was that Craig, like his mother, was determined no one would push him around. When Gilman suggested the taxi squad, Craig said nothing doing unless he was to receive full salary. That was not Sid Gilman's idea of a good deal so he let Craig go. There were no tears, nor any sad songs on Craig's part then. He was not bitter, either. He was plain angry. Goddamn it, he kept telling me, you'll be reading my name in the papers yet! As for me, he just felt sorry for me, with nobody to throw to now except those "two other cats."

And I did hear about Craig Cotton too, for he landed with Detroit and right away earned attention for his hustle, his range and the ferocity of his play. And one time I heard the announcer at a Detroit game report: "Coach Joe Schmidt thinks he has a real find in Craig Cotton. He is most impressed with his hard-working attitude. He thinks that, with Cotton, he has two of the finest young tight ends in the business." (The other one is Charlie Sanders, who is surely one of the best.) Just like Craig said, I heard about him!

I got to see Craig again, too, by accident, and without

warning, right here in the National Guard. I was wandering about Fort Ord one afternoon, feeling lonely, trying to look busy, or at least awake, when a group of green-clad guys came by, doing their physical-training jog. One tall black guy was out front—and it was Craig! I let out a yell. Craig stopped and suddenly Fort Ord became not half so lousy a spot as it had been up until then to both of us. From then on, we worked out together often. Craig was his old bubbling self, the heavy rapper, the eternal optimist, Sid Gilman, he declared, had helped him more than anyone, had taught him more about playing tight end than he had learned in Detroit, and had done him a great favor in turning him loose to sign with the Lions. And one of these days soon, Craig promised me, he'd be Number One tight end, and no more specialty teams! (As for those "two other cats," MacKinnon was last seen on the Oakland cab squad and Frazier, after a mediocre year with the Chargers, was shipped off to Houston.)

But the point I wanted to make about Craig was that he never let his being black divert him from whatever goal he sought, whether it was an evening with one of the San Diego dazzlers or a job as first-string tight end on a pro football team.

It may be true that on other clubs there is active racism. There are, God knows, one or two guys on our coaching staff who could practice that religion if they were in different surroundings. And sometimes you hear one of our Confederates trying to play the part of the unreconstructed rebel by growling about "niggers" and repeating some petty libel about a black player—when all the blacks are out of earshot. Some of the blacks too will try to persuade you that the Chargers are determined not to let a black man play wide receiver. I don't believe this. We just haven't had, so far, a black player who has been good enough in that position. And I can't imagine Sid Gilman turning down a Gene Washington, for instance, if he ever found such a prize in his Christmas stocking.

What form our subdued racism does take is in stupid and thoughtless reactions by some of the coaching staff. If, for instance, when we visit another city, a crew of obvious hookers should appear in our hotel lobby, as they often do, there is one coach who will *always* assume that the black players brought them there, and he will single out a black player or two to "warn" against such flagrant carryings-on. You know, black men being oversexed, and all! Ignorant behavior of this sort irritates everybody. Anyway, who says that only the blacks are All-Pro in the stud department?

Up to date anyway, I have seen none of the discrimination that is supposed to have been practiced on other clubs. Perhaps it has been driven underground and out of sight —and that's all to the good. Blacks and whites in our club live together, play together, and relax together. And I hope that one day there will be a world like that.

No doubt it is true that Craig Cotton, coming from a really well-to-do background, grew up with a minimum of prejudice around him, and suffered none of the more vicious forms of discrimination. But there are other black men like him and some day there could be a country full of them. He did not feel he was being dehumanized by pro football any more than I do. The game thrilled him. The hard hitting never scared him. And there was far more satisfaction for him in accomplishing a good play on the field than just the thought of the money he might earn.

2

Hail, Columbia

At the risk of making it all sound like an ego trip, I think I had better back off for a few minutes and explain how it happened that I, who never had any such goal in mind when I started playing football, wound up being drafted Number One by the San Diego Chargers. I became a quarterback by accident—through losing my temper in public—and I developed the pro football urge very gradually indeed.

My background has no weirdo parents in it, no orphanage or drunken stepfather, no conniving high school coach, no "search for identity," whatever the hell that is. I was never beaten up or called nasty names by my classmates, nor was I neglected by my father.

My father, who is now a teacher, was a hard-working and successful printer when I was growing up, a religious man who attended mass every Sunday and taught his progeny to do the same, and a man who provided a comfortable and loving home for all of us—three sisters and me. (Now there is an extra one, a three-year-old brother, so I can't even include a broken home in the script.) My father believed in education. He did not drive us or grind us down. But he expected us to do well in our studies and was no man to accept lightly any "low" marks (below 90) in school. There was neither drink nor neglect in our household. The whiskey bottle stayed on a shelf in the kitchen except when we had company. There were always baseball bats in the garage, a football in the closet, and a basket—a basketball basket, that is—in the yard. My

17

father had a lifelong addiction to sports and coached me in Little League baseball when I was small. My mother, who has only a superficial knowledge of competitive games, apparently voted in favor of sports because they kept me out of the house.

So I played baseball, basketball, and football, and my father still insists that baseball is my best sport. But being big and strong, I favored football and played in the Pop Warner League before I went to Christian Brothers Academy in my home town of Syracuse. I was always a lineman—guard, tackle, and finally end. Del Shofner, the great receiver of the New York Giants, was my secret model. Never at any time, before I went to college, did I carry pictures in my head of Marty Domres tearing up the turf at Yankee Stadium—or even at San Diego Stadium. Like every other healthy and self-centered teenager, I lived for the immediate moment.

There were no really great moments in my Academy career, but there were a number I'll never forget. We played in the rough, tough Central New York League, where there were plenty of guys as big as I was and many a whole lot tougher. By the time I reached the Academy I had settled for playing end, where I relished most the grabbing of long passes and sprinting downfield for scores. But I was playing for the Junior Varsity and my immediate ambition was to prove myself worthy of the big team. There was just one guy who stood in my way—Rick Cavallaro. Rick did not play end. He was the quarterback. He was a damn good quarterback too. He had just one fault—he could not pass a football worth a shit. So my dream of winning varsity status through snagging touchdown passes faded in a volley of overthrown, underthrown, and just badly thrown footballs. When Rick was not bouncing the ball on the ground ten yards short of me, he was heaving it far over the sideline, or delivering a wobbly pass into the hands of the enemy.

I became a quarterback because I lost my temper in the big game of our six-game season, the game against Nottingham. More than any other goal in life, we dearly desired to clobber this outfit. I know it shouldn't have been so, but it was. Nottingham had a large Jewish enrollment and we were, of course, Roman Catholic. So, being very devout little Catholics, we hated Nottingham to death and charged ourselves up to the blow-off point with the urge to demolish them.

Nottingham must have come to the game with the same attitude, for, after we had got off to a long lead, they battled us back until there was only a touchdown between us. At this point I begged Rick Cavallaro to throw me the ball because I was beating my coverage seven ways from St. Louis. So Rick called what passed in our circles for a "square out" and I left my defender far behind. Whereupon Rick bounced the ball on the turf five yards to my rear. In the huddle I urged Rick to try again, my defender being so easy to deal with. So Rick called the same play—and this time he delivered the ball to a spot some five yards ahead of me and out of bounds. Well, I reasoned, the guy has me straddled, so he is bound to zero in on the third try.

Whatever gave me that idea, I don't know. Rick called the play again and this time I beat my defender so badly that the poor slob fell right on his face. I could have trotted backward over the goal line—if only I could get hold of the ball. But good old Rick came up short again, bouncing the ball several long strides away. I fielded the ball on the bounce, so thoroughly pissed off and frustrated that I could not stifle my anger. Without thought, I gripped the damn football tight and fired it full force right back at Rick Cavallaro. Rick put up both hands to protect himself. The ball split his hands, hit him square on the forehead, and sent him staggering. We lost that game. But on Monday, on the strength of my rocket-like delivery of the ball to Cavallaro, I was named quarterback. And I have been a quarterback ever since.

The rest of my career at the Academy held no such high drama. I did well enough but won no great amount of ink nor any throng of college recruiters. We tied twice for championships and about all I accomplished that was notable was to complete more touchdown passes than any of my rivals in that league. In my junior year I received letters from thirty schools or so, none of them really beseeching me to come play for them—just the standard letters asking height and weight, my scholastic average, and inquiring about my college plans. Several of the major football factories, like Penn State and Syracuse, had me on their mailing list but, on the urging of my father and mother, I eliminated them immediately from consideration. Nor did anyone from those plants show up on my doorstep to pressure me.

Ultimately, I worked the possibilities down to six— Columbia, Brown, Pennsylvania, Dartmouth, Hobart, and Buffalo. Why Hobart? And why Buffalo? Well, Hobart was close by and the coach, Alva Kelly, pointed out to me the advantages of being a big, or medium-sized, frog in a small puddle. As for Buffalo, they were setting out to build themselves to major college status but were not yet big time, and there too I might find the competition less severe.

What finally decided me was, I think, the attitudes and personalities of the different coaches and recruiters I talked to. I liked everything about Buff Donelli, who was then coach at Columbia. He quite obviously thought of me as a person, and not just a slab of meat to fill a hole in the line-up. His interest was sincere and thorough. Besides, he took care not to downgrade any of the other schools I was considering. He simply urged me, for the sake of my own future, to select an Ivy League school, where I was certain of an education. And if I came to Columbia, I was assured that one of the coaches would be directly responsible for my well being in school, particularly for my staying up to standard in my academic work. A Columbia education, and a Columbia degree, meant money in the bank to a student, Donelli argued. But if I decided against Columbia, he still wanted me to choose a school where education came first.

Some of the other guys really turned me off. There was a Dartmouth alumnus who applied the real hard sell, as if he were trying to unload a used car before the fenders fell off. "Yes or no, son!" he kept insisting. "Just yes or no!" And in between times he declared that anyone who could choose another school ahead of Dartmouth had to be off his rocker.

Contrasted to him was Hubie Schultz, Columbia '38, who was just so damn honest, so sincere, and so obviously in love with his Alma Mater that there was no resisting him. He had several hundred anecdotes of college life to relate that would have cracked up even Andrei Gromyko, so infectious was his own laughter.

And then there was the guy assigned to steer me about the Columbia campus—as other recruiters had "shown" me the campuses of their universities. This was Tom Chorba, a completely off-the-wall character who knew Columbia and its environs, from Greenwich Village to Baker Field, as no other man alive could have known them. He was no football hero, no politician, no aging glamour boy—just a real hot shit who could charm the billy club off a campus cop. Never, in walking to and fro around Columbia, did we pass a pretty girl who did not know Tom. Nor was there a recreation spot in the city that Tom could not find his way about.

Tom was totally frank—so refreshing after my several doses of alumni stuffed-shirtism that he took my breath away. Tom knew what a healthy young guy was *really* interested in about the town he would have to live in and he made sure I saw everything. He introduced me to Lincoln Center, to Radio City Music Hall, to Carnegie Hall, to restaurants of every flavor. Who the hell, I wondered (and still wonder), could select the hills of old New Hampshire after one real good look at New York!

So I chose Clumbia. And despite the fact that my football career there shows just six wins out of 27 games, I have never regretted it. If they offered me a rerun, I'd take Columbia again. Maybe if Dave Meggyesey had done that, he'd never have had to turn to pot to make life bearable.

Playing football at Columbia was—I mean it—*fun*. Even the practice sessions—especially the practice sessions!— were satisfying to my soul. I was almost always the first player out for practice and would fill in time before the session by playing two-hand touch with the neighborhood kids who always gathered to watch the workout. I was never conscious of any gimlet-eyed coaches bent on brutalizing my nature, of any leering alumni with side-money to offer me, or of advisers who would undertake to keep me from wasting too much time on classroom work. By the lights of coach Frank Navarro, who succeeded Donelli, and in keeping with his own expressed belief, young athletes came to Columbia for an education and it was his responsibility to see that they received it.

My parents were pleased with my choice naturally, and the whole family would drive down to attend the games I played in. (My mother, who could not stand to see me courting a broken neck this way, would always walk out before the game was over.)

Out of all the games I played, there are two that I like to dwell on, not just because I did well in them, but because they provided me with a satisfaction that so far in my life only football has given. No doubt the emotion they stirred in me was corny. Undoubtedly the build-up to the games was partially juvenile, or at least adolescent, and the "triumph" we sought was fairy-tale. But goddamn it, it was all real enough to me then—as real as young love, and my first taste of religion, and the joys I find in many of life's illusions, such as music, and art, and purple skies and blue oceans.

Columbia had not beaten Princeton since nobody could recall exactly when—at least twenty years. And we did not rate a chance to beat them in my last year at Columbia either. But the fact that the other guy was the overwhelming favorite never once, in all the time I played at Columbia, kept us from going into a game looking for victory. We *always* planned to win, one way or another. If we could not outman the enemy, we tried to outscheme him, or get him off balance, or just fight him to death on the field.

But when we came to play the Tigers in Palmer Stadium, Princeton was a twenty-point favorite. *Everybody* looked for Princeton to push us out of the park—everybody except our coaches and the team. *We* really thought we might win —by getting hold of the ball and throwing the hell out of it, until we got a lead we could hang on to. And the 30,000 or more people who came to watch the game saw us come close to doing just that. It was Homecoming Weekend and we were the sacrificial offering, as we had been for a couple of decades. Only this time, we told ourselves, we would do the celebrating.

So we threw and threw. And we turned what was supposed to be a rout into a football game. After three and a half quarters, the score was Princeton 17, Columbia 10, and the game was still within our reach. Naturally, with us concentrating on passing, I had been taking a heavy drubbing all afternoon. After the game, I learned I had been decked 58 times—many times, of course, after the ball had been released. But at this point in the struggle, when I could still smell victory, I had no thought for bruises. We had the ball on our twenty and if we could score, and go for a two-point conversion, we could take the lead. Every damn one of us played in a frenzy then, and we passed, scrambled, and slugged until we had gone the full eighty yards for the score. Then we tried for the two points on a pass. But a really great play by one of the Princeton defensive backs beat the ball to the ground and we were one point behind.

This did not lick us completely, but it marked the point where the game suddenly turned around. Princeton took the following kickoff all the way back to add seven points to their lead and we promptly found ourselves on our own twenty-yard line again needing eight points just to tie.

We went after them too and with any kind of breaks we should have had them. But when we got down to the Princeton ten-yard line some lucky-ass son of a bitch in black and orange grabbed hold of a bobbled pass and ran off with it. How the hell I ever caught him I don't know. I was just goddamned if I'd let him score. I hit him on our 23-yard line and brought him down. But by this time we were pooped—outmanned and outgunned in every way and no longer able to even the balance on sheer emotion. In one play the Tigers made the whole 23 yards to score and we were down fifteen.

Every one of us by this time—and I think me most of

all—had been bruised and battered and bumped until there
was an ache in every bone. But we were still determined to
make it close at least, to get one more score on the board
before the gun. So back we went and tried to act as if
we still had the strength to do it. But the juices had gone
dry. We had been sitting disconsolate on the bench, ready
to weep, after that final Princeton score. Now fatigue had
us by the throat.

The crowd was all pulling for us now, just because we
had put on such a show. But it did not help. We completed
two passes, and I scrambled for six yards to get back into
Princeton territory. After the scramble I found I could
hardly get to my feet and it seemed to take me ten minutes
to reach the huddle. Well, one more completion might do
it and I was determined to try. So we tried. My weary—
and always outmatched—protectors just could not hold off
the rush this time and I never had a chance to get the ball
away. Those bright-eyed and rosy-cheeked Princeton substitutes were all panting in upon me in a flash. I managed
to dodge the first man and take off around right end, ducking Princeton defenders at every step. As I crossed the
scrimmage line I managed to elude a linebacker by cutting
back into the middle. Promptly I was belted from the rear
by still another defensive man. I staggered and spun away.
And just as I completed my spin there was one more
defensive back leaping at me. He "stood me up" with a
jar like banging face first into a wall. And at once I saw
every Princeton player on the field, all eleven of them,
piling in to get a crack at me. When I finally hit the sodden
turf I felt as if I was going to stay there a long time. Yet
crushed beneath the pack, with my ribs begging for mercy,
I remember hearing the tremendous moan the crowd gave
out, as if they had felt the shattering impact of that gang
tackle in their own frames. There was a whistle—maybe
six whistles for all I know. The 82d Airborne gradually
climbed off my twisted corpse. I looked wearily up into
the alarmed faces of Coach Navarro and the trainer, who
had sprinted out onto the field as soon as they saw me
collapse.

Smelling salts chased the fog from my brain and in a

few seconds I was able to get up and make my way off the field with just a single shoulder to lean on. And that is when I got my reward—a thundering ovation that smashed down upon me like Yellowstone Falls, as if from a thousand yards above. Every damn soul in that stadium, friend and enemy alike, must have been clapping and yelling. My teammates all stood in a rank along the sidelines, pounding their hands and yelling God knows what. I could see all the frenzied mouths working. Inside me something let go and I started to cry, until the tears cut two wide streaks on my face. I sat down on the bench and put my face in my hands. The cheers continued and kept resounding until the final gun.

Then I dragged myself into the locker room and dropped in front of my locker, still weeping. Hands reached out to shake mine. The Princeton coach came by and said something about it being the greatest performance he had ever seen. But nothing registered. I sat there, completely done in, pissed, frustrated, and inconsolable. All I knew was that the lousy fucking Princeton bastards had won the *ball* game! Who would ever make up for that? Even when the radio on the way home gave out with more praise— and when the whole busload of my teammates cheered the mention of my name, I still felt no thrill.

It was not until next day that I began to savor some of the satisfactions. It had been like a one-man war. I had thrown 53 passes and completed 28, two of them for touchdowns, for a total gain through the air of 354 yards. I had scrambled twenty times for another forty yards. Out of Columbia's 84 plays from scrimmage I had handled the ball all but eleven times. So call me conceited. But I had taken the worst physical hammering of my whole life and I felt entitled to dwell for a while on the few things I had done that were good.

The other game that I still like to set my memory wallowing in also took place in my senior year, against Cornell. When we came to that game, we had yet to win one and hardly anybody thought we would come out ahead this time either. There was added excitement all week because the pro scouts had been smelling around regularly. Several of them were always on hand for practice and this added to the gradual build-up of tension. The coach, God bless him, would not let scouts talk to a player on the field or in the field house. But I knew they were timing my drop-off, watching my delivery, quizzing the coaches. Day by day the pressure increased.

On the Saturday of the game I arrived extra early at Baker Field, hoping for a chance to loosen the tension. From a corner of the field house I watched the soccer game with Cornell, so far off I could not identify all the players. Idly I waited as our team bus pulled up to let the rest of the guys off and I walked in with the last group. I could feel my breath already getting a little short.

Bill Wazewich, my best receiver, walked out with me after we had suited up, and I inspected the playing surface. This is a ritual I go through even now, before every game. On the field I walked past a group of scouts and swapped greetings. So they would all be here to watch every damn move I made! Back to the field house then to wait some more, then out on the field with the whole squad for warm-ups. Those scouts! I could not put them out of my mind as I went through all the familiar moves. When the warm-up was over I was almost gasping for breath.

In the field house once more we made some last-minute adjustments. The problems had been the same all season—not enough depth, not enough line blocking, invariable fatigue in the final quarter. So again it would be chiefly passing from whistle to whistle. Coach Navarro gave us a pep-talk—a little more feeling in this one, for *we had* to win this game or count the whole season a disaster. When he gave us the final "Go out and get 'em!" the room really exploded. The squad roared out the door in a stampede. As usual, I followed last, still trying to get my breath. On the way to the field my parents and friends were waiting to pat me and wish me luck. Now suddenly my breath surged back and I felt charged up and eager to lay my hands on the ball!

Cornell received the first kickoff and moved quickly for a score. We took the ball then and soon had the tying touchdown. Then we scored again and hung on to a lead.

Late in the third quarter, our defense began to weaken. Cornell scored a touchdown and went ahead 26 to 25. This seemed like a rerun of so many other games—a hard struggle, a slim lead, and then a narrow defeat. But we told ourselves we *couldn't* let this happen again. At the opening of the fourth quarter, our defense, self-inspired in the huddle, held Cornell for downs on our own eight. It was the last chance now, first down and 92 yards to go to our first victory.

Our other backs were really dragging their asses, having run and run all afternoon on pass patterns of every conceivable depth and design. So I was going to have to pass the ball or hang on to it—or give up any hope. My first pass took the ball to our own 20. Another pass and we reached the 35. Two running plays made just four yards. On third and six there was no choice but to pass again. So I called a pass and the Cornell defense covered our receivers as if they had all come to the game together. Once more I had to break out of the pocket and scramble for passing room, hoping to God someone would tear loose. Then by God our big tight end broke free far down field and I hit him in stride for a fifty-yard gain.

We were stalled for a time but now we were close enough to score a field goal that put us two points ahead. Not enough! We had to have that ball back and score again. With a lead to set their teeth into, our beat-up defense held tight again and we got the ball back with just three minutes left. Pass, scramble, pass, scramble (no one else seemed to have strength left even to get over the scrimmage line). But eventually we brought the ball to the Cornell 37, where they got their backs up. Two plays netted us nine yards. It was third and one. The Cornell defense, just as I hoped, stacked to stop the run. I was almost snickering with anticipation as I called a play-action pass. It worked like a motion picture. The fake pulled in the defense and Bill Wazewich broke loose with no one between him and the goal. I faded back and let fly, a high soft pass that settled like a leaf in Bill's hands in perfect stride. He trotted over the goal line and bounced the ball ten feet in the air. The stands roared as if they had been set off by a fuse and people just seemed to melt down onto the field and overrun it.

Suddenly I realized that, for Christ's sake, I had actually *forgotten* about the scouts! We had our first victory: 34-26. I turned to look where the scouts might be and grinned in their direction. The Cornell coach, Jack Musick, was suddenly at my side, solemn and earnest, shaking my hand. A lot of guys were grabbing at me and I made no effort to escape but let them hoist me to their shoulders and trot me off, held high above the crowd, while hands kept reaching out for me.

The whole week after that was Ego Week for me. Handshakes and smiles and kisses, people yelling to me wherever I showed my face. My picture, for God's sake, in *Sports Illustrated*, which named me Back of the Week. It was as if there had never been any defeats, or any bruises, or any passes knocked astray, or any gang tackles, or any deckings. The very air tasted sweet as apple juice and I walked about the campus, and through the familiar downtown haunts, as if I had a golden cloud around me. Now *this* was the way it was *supposed* to be! It is one of the things men play football for!

I took the statistics out from time to time and privately gloried in them: Total gains 447 yards, 396 passing and 51 scrambling. Three touchdown passes. No interceptions, 25 completions out of 42 attempts. Okay, pro scouts, write *those* down!

Well, that seems long ago and now I am back almost where I began, only with tougher and meaner opposition and more pressure to execute properly. Clippings and college statistics impress no one now—not even me. What I cling to is that wonderful soul-filling satisfaction that came when that football settled in Bill Wazewich's hands and I *knew* I had finally done the job.

3

On Blood, Drugs, Booze, and Broads

What about this blood and gore bit—this theory that pro football brings out the worst in all our natures, that it is the modern form of the Roman Circuses, and that we are the gladiators—or are we sometimes the damn lions? I try to be open-minded when I hear such talk. I know as well as anybody that there are a number of jocks who have got their training in the football factories and who have been 100 percent "physical" all their lives. But I don't know anyone who really relishes doing another guy a serious injury. Most men get a kick out of hard hitting. And it is also true that many a guy, in the fight to hold his job, deals out some bitter blows and takes measures to subdue his own pain during the contest. But when a guy is really racked up, with a broken leg or an injury more serious, almost everyone feels kind of sick about it.

The first time I saw (and heard) a leg broken on the field is a moment I am not going to forget. It happened in Fullerton, when we were scrimmaging the Rams, and one of the sorry things is that I can't even recall the guy's name—some guy who had come up from the Ram taxi squad and had been doing real well. In the scrimmage, we would run ten plays and they would run ten plays. We had tried one play through the line and the coach wanted us to run it again. So I called it once more in the huddle, we lined up, and as I handed off I heard this really shattering noise—a resounding *craaack!* It was the noise a two-by-four makes if you lay it across two sawhorses and jump on it, breaking it in two. I thought at once, what a hell of a hit! It seemed to me that two shoulder pads had met full-tilt to make that noise. But I looked down and saw one of the Rams on the ground with one of his own men fallen across his leg. The man on the ground tried to lift his leg as the other guy got off him. But the lower part of his shin just sagged down, across the grain. Both bones had obviously been broken clean across.

"Ahhh God!" the man screamed. "My leg! My leg!"

The men with the first aid kits came sprinting across the field and they got all the rest of us out of there. After his first scream, the poor guy just lay there, his face so contorted he looked like someone else, and he growled a long stream of obscenities. The rest of us, looking back at him, and looking at each other, just shook our heads. I know I was not the only one who moved for the sidelines, afraid of throwing up. Jesus, what a sickening sound!

They gave the guy a shot of some sort to ease the pain and took him off the field. There was no rejoicing by our side, or by anybody watching. It took us all several minutes actually to get back into the spirit of the scrimmage. Both sides were a little subdued for the next few plays and believe me I was grateful for the big red cross I wore on my chest and back as a sign I was not to be hit. Nobody in scrimmage is allowed to hit the quarterback.

There was an injury in pre-season too, to Bob Babich, my new roommate. Bob, a rookie linebacker, was touted among the coaches as another Butkus or Nobis, a free-ranging, hard-hitting crowd-pleaser. Against the Oakland Raiders, in pre-season at Oakland, Bob played a hell of a game and helped us hold the Raiders to one touchdown and beat them. He seemed a cinch to make first string. But when we played Cleveland, in the very first quarter, someone belted him full across the legs and tore up one of his knees. This was not a noisy injury. But everyone, on both sides, knew it was serious. A knee injury is what every player dreads most, because it can mean no more football. A guy has to have an immediate operation, lots of luck, and incredible determination to come back if his knee ligaments are torn. When they carried Bob off the field, the fans gave him a long tribute of applause. But every man on the bench was absolutely silent and glum, almost as if they had carried his dead body off. No rejoicing there, no celebrating the destruction of an enemy.

I don't believe fans satisfy any blood-lust at football games either, or get some vicarious thrill at seeing young fellows get their bones shattered, their veins opened, or their brains scrambled. It is true fans will yell in excitement and joy at a solid hit—a tackle that takes a runner clean off his feet or spins him into the air, a solid block that wipes out a potential tackler, a head-on collision that pops a football loose. But they yell not because they think anyone has been hurt, but out of a combination of fear and amazement—amazement that any man can give or take a blow so fierce.

They will scream even harder and get far more excited if a man breaks free far downfield, grasps a thrown football in his fingertips, and sprints all the way to the goal line without anyone touching him at all. What the fans pray for and cheer for and go into fits of hysteria about are the scores, and above all the victories. They will bellow and jump up and down and run screaming onto the field if the victory comes from a 50-yard field goal, or even a recovered fumble, or a bad pass from center. They don't need to see blood. They just need to win.

Besides, a fan watching from the stands does not really savor the brutality of the game as it is played along the scrimmage line, where guys wallop the enemy with hands and forearms, or spear them with their helmets. From a distance, the line play is almost soundless and seems just a well-drilled maneuver, like the lunging forward of a ballet line. Its being full of hard contact makes it more exciting. But it does not set anybody to watering at the mouth for the sight of blood.

Players do relish good hard contact and there is solid satisfaction in a sharp block that moves an enemy right out of the play, or in a tackle that brings a runner down as if he had been clubbed. But it is the accomplishment that thrills you, along with the knowledge that you have taken a long stride toward victory. If two teams take to walloping each other, or get too busy dealing out excess punishment in the pit, the fans will soon get fed up. They want *scores*, not blood and broken bones. The scores being secured at some bodily risk make them that much dearer.

I had no serious hurts at all in my first season but in my second pre-season, against New Orleans, I really bought myself a bad sprain. It was a weird feeling to *know* you are going to get hurt, to feel knee and ankle yielding slowly, slowly, to severe pressure and to actually anticipate the sickening pop when the ligaments on either side of the ankle go.

We had a real offense going when it happened too, so it was all the more frustrating and disheartening. Old "Golden Wheels" Foster, our fullback (somebody in his home town had sent him a pair of gold-colored shoes) had taken the ball on the first play I called and carried it for thirty yards.

We were behind then 14 to 17. John Hadl, having had a slow first half, I replaced him in the third quarter and on my first call I found the Saints aligned just as I had expected—so I was feeling well charged up at the play's success. My next call was a roll-out, with the backs faking one way while I went the other, and "Y," the tight end, cut straight across.

But the Saints got to me quickly. I was shoved, had to run, and about seven or eight yards downfield found a safety man waiting. I tried to put a move on him but he was not impressed. Instead he laid his shoulder into me and set out to throw me over backward. I don't believe he'd have made it, I being so much bigger, but the defensive end immediately hit me from behind, right across the legs. Immediately I was being pressed both ways, my knees and ankles buckling and being forced backward at the same time. I must have struggled some but it seemed to me that I just lay in that human vise staring up at the Sugar Bowl lights and felt the pressure grow and grow until the ligaments popped. It was the popping sensation more than the pain that sent the shivers through me. Afterward Charley Waller, who had been promoted to head coach, said I had looked as if I had a broken back, the way I thrashed about trying to free my legs and find some footing. I came to my feet, with the adrenalin pouring through my veins in such quantity that I actually felt I could shake this incident off. The crowd roared to see me get up and I started to trot back to position. I trotted but one step. My ankle gave out beneath me as if the foot had been chopped off, and down I went in a shapeless heap. I had to be lifted and carried to the sidelines.

But once there I felt neither rage at the enemy nor terror at what might befall me next. Instead I was almost weeping with frustration. I wanted to *play!* And some voice deep in my brain kept telling me that this was the end, that there would be no more football, that an injury like this would never heal.

So I knew then why men who seem half torn apart, who wear yards of bandage and tape over bleeding limbs, or who need shots to keep from wincing with pain at every step—why they insist on getting back into the action.

The New Orleans Saints are what we call a "physical" team. That is, they try to make up for lack of skills by going all out to hit hard and hurt the opposition—not to injure you, just to make you feel the blows and perhaps cause you to cringe a little and try to avoid contact next time. Sid Gilman had often expressed his opinion of their roster as being made up of cast-offs, misfits, and retreads who would never have stayed in the league had it not been for expansion. This open-eyed appraisal of their talents had undoubtedly been repeated to the Saints a dozen times or more as their coaches endeavored to build up that blood-lust some leaders require in all their charges. So when the Chargers and the Saints met in battle—even in sham battle—there was always plenty of late-hitting, plenty of dirty names, plenty of challenges to single combat.

I was surprised at the venom the Saints poured out on us in this game. And I had been puzzled and amused by Sid Gilman's habit, as we went over the film of the Saints in action, of constantly referring to Steve Stonebreaker, the Saints linebacker, as "the horseshit middle linebacker." Then one of my teammates enlightened me.

The year before I came to the Chargers, a fight had broken out in the Saints-Chargers game and Sid, after watching the men on both sides vainly trying to slip punches through each other's face masks, had rushed out on the field shouting "Break it up! Break it up!" Stonebreaker, perhaps unduly exhilarated by the appearance of a target without a mask, immediately detached himself from the riot and belted poor Sid in the face. "The most bitchin' sucker shot ever seen, man!"

Down went Sid. And out on the field roared Ron Billingsley, defensive lineman, six-feet-eight and 290 pounds, determined to avenge his beloved coach. But he had hardly crossed the line when two Saints jumped him, grounded him, and pinned his arms to the sod. Ron raised his head to the full length of his neck and tried to explain that he just wanted to even things up for his coach.

"And you know what?" Ron told me, wide-eyed. "That motherfucker just hit me right up side the head, without me having a chance! Can you *imagine!*"

When some people talk about "drugs" in pro athletics they mean something altogether different from pot or skag or hash or the other commodities that they might relish themselves. They mean pain-killing drugs that are used, supposedly, by corrupt and conniving trainers and doctors to enable them to push severely injured men back into the fray. Well, I have never seen anyone on our club shove a man back into a game when he was unable and unwilling to continue. I have seen weeping and cursing men restrained from going back. And I have seen men with head injuries who are positive they are "all right" still held out of action by the trainer until they have had a thorough examination by the team physician.

There are several players on our squad who will conceal injuries or pain so that they will not be lifted. One of the toughest men who ever lived is Walt Sweeney, who suffered a severe sprain of an ankle in the New Orleans preseason game and who insisted he felt no pain at all. When the trainer tried to examine it Sweeney told him to stay the hell away or "you'll need a trainer yourself, you stupid

obscene descendant of a dirty word!" On the Tuesday after
the game, when his ankle actually hurt to look at, Walt
was running again. He asked for a pain-killer, then started
and finished the Baltimore game, the season opener. I
know damn well the drug could only have had a minor
effect on the pain Walt felt. But he never winced, nor
favored the bad ankle once.

Another tough cookie is Bob Bruggers, who had a
thumb broken in a league game and refused to be removed
from his linebacker job. He never complained—except to
ask that he be given a more flexible cast, which would have
slowed up the healing but would have enabled him to play
more effectively. He was more worried about the tackles
he missed than he was about a possible re-injury.

Then there is Pete Barnes, who suffers from what he
calls "bad fuckin' feet." Every time he leaves practice he
moves with a sort of painful hippity-hop that everybody
calls the "Barnes shuffle." But very seldom does anyone
hear him bitch and only once or twice has he taken a day
off to rest his suffering wheels.

Russ Smith too is a man who plays in pain at his own
insistence and with no complaints. When the trainer has
finished taping and bandaging Russ preparatory to his
going into a game, Russ looks as if he had been dug out of
an Egyptian tomb. But you'd never know to watch his effort on the field that he felt even a twinge.

These are tough men who like to play football and like
to win. Nobody is driving or drugging them into facing
the enemy, any more than they had to frighten Sandy
Koufax into pitching baseball games when his arm tortured
him. Men like this have an inner drive that no pain can
stifle—and no drug can replace. It is not a conspiracy
among doctors and trainers nor the result of slave-driving
by the coach. It is the way some men are made, and I
don't believe it signifies anything wicked or anti-social in
our natures.

It is part of the game to try to hit hard enough to make
a man hesitate about running into you again. It is part of
other games besides football. Even in baseball, the second-
baseman or shortstop who flinches from contact when

making a putout can count on getting more and more of it. It is a good feeling to meet a man as strong and big as yourself, to meet him head on, and not chicken out. Fierce physical contact does of course produce anger at times, especially if it seems needless or overdone. There are players who rough an opponent up just to make him lose his cool and perhaps get himself penalized or tossed out of the game. God knows others besides the New Orleans Saints are decidedly unsaintly in their readiness to start throwing punches. But most of this on-the-field anger, most of the dirty-bastard, fuck-you exchanges are washed right off with the final whistle and no resentment at all is left. (It has to be that way in professional sports, where you may find the "dirty bastard" and yourself on the same side one day.)

Everybody who comes into pro football knows he is going to get this "physical" treatment. It is part of the initiation of quarterbacks. I had my bell rung most resoundingly in my first season when I took over at quarterback against the Kansas City Chiefs. I had hardly got used to being on the field when Buck Buchanan roared into me from my blind side and with one fearsome clout of his taped-up forearm sent my heels flying higher than my helmet. It was a full minute before the chimes in my head quieted enough for me to hear any other sound. I looked up and saw Buck grinning down at me.

"Welcome to the American League!" he said.

In my second year, at Denver, I received one real clobbering which, while not sidelining me for any length of time, did ring my bell just as roundly as Buck Buchanan's greeting had the year before. It was third down and 21 to go on our own ten-yard line. I decided the best play to take advantage of the Denver pass-rush was a reverse by the tight end that would have him taking the toss at "eight" —the outside hole on the right. The Denver defensive ends always rushed to the outside and this play was designed to fake them out completely. I faked a hand-off to the fullback, who thereupon set out to hit the defensive tackle with an "isolation block." I faked to the running back, who hit full speed into the "four" hole (between

right guard and tackle). Then I was to pitch out to tight
tight end. But the Denver defense completely ignored all
the fakes and blasted right through. Jackson, their big
defensive end, charged straight at me, while the left linebacker blew in and took away the pitch-out. I stood and
tried to put on a fake of some sort but Jackson simply
clouted me on the head with his hand and forearm, sending me down.

Before I had even settled into the ground (I have not
yet learned how to curl up in the fetal position, the way
Fran Tarkenton does), Smith, the other end, struck me.
He landed right on my face guard with his knee. It was
like being hit there with the blunt end of a telephone pole.
My face guard and helmet cracked under the pressure and
cut my lip severely.

As I lay on the ground, my throat filled quickly with
blood and I spat it out in a gob that flew up out of my
mouth to the height of more than a foot, horrifying one
or two onlookers. I got up quickly then, fearful I might
strangle, and staggered backward until I hit the goal posts.
I spun around then and hit the ground once more. That
was all the football I played that day. But my instincts
were to get back into the play, to shake it off, to make up
for what we had lost.

Nearly every young man making his start in a muscular
profession, whether it be soccer, basketball, bronco bust-
ing, baseball, or bricklaying, is likely to run into some sort
of breaking-in ceremony. There are some civilizations that
have used a proof-of-manhood initiation rite for centuries,
with the candidate required to illustrate his ability to with-
stand pain. So I am not going to line up with the people
who try to tell you that the brutality of pro football is
turning us all into sub-human monsters whose knuckles
scrape the turf when we walk.

What is dehumanizing about pro football, probably more
than most professional athletics, is the control over a man's
life exercised not just by the coach but by club owners,
sports writers, and broadcasters. With people publicly ap-
praising your market worth and your chances of being
swapped off for two defensive men, plus your real inability,

despite the "option" clause, to find your own market for your services, you begin sometimes to feel like a hunk of meat. Add to this the tight control of your sleeping and drinking schedule and the threat of even more intimate delving into your off-hour doings and you can begin to picture yourself as a dumb creature tied in a stall.

One of the clauses of our contract permits the management to demand a urine sample whenever it strikes them as proper. I never gave this much mind until one game when I actually had been doing pretty well. But at one point Coach Waller sent Walker Gillette, our rookie receiver, into the game with a play. Walker's broad hillbilly accent, plus his breathless excitement, made it just about impossible for him to get the words out in a form that I could understand. After three vain attempts had eaten away most of the seconds allowed, I called time and walked over to get the word straight from Waller.

"What's the matter?" Charley demanded. "Did you take something before the game?" I brushed that off, got the play, and went back to work. We scored a lot of points. But as we reviewed the films of the game, Charley kept offering negative remarks. (In his own lingo, learned at a special course in leadership or something, these could be called "negative rocks"—as opposed to "positive rocks" that were supposed to tip the balance the right way.) "What did you do that for?" "You didn't hand off right!" he would growl from time to time.

Then the film showed one play in which I was knocked off balance. As I went down, I managed to get off an underhand toss to the fullback and he made a 24-yard gain. Charley snorted. "That's an old Ivy League play," he said.

I was so damn mad by then that my palms were actually sweating. But there was more.

"You know," Charley went on, in a solemn tone, "I'm going to have to get a urine sample from you after one of these games!"

Maybe Charley was feeling extra touchy about any sort of "inspired" actions, because at that time defensive tackle Houston Ridge was suing the club, accusing it of feeding him drugs to increase his viciousness and deaden his pain.

But the comments Charley was feeding me were prompting a few vicious notions in my own mind and I nearly came back with an offer to provide a sample when he least looked for it.

Despite dressing downs from coaches, the sprains and the cuts and the occasional dizzying whacks on the head, football was still fun for most of us. The discipline was tighter than in the National Guard. But you can't make much money in the Guard. And I imagine that, in a number of other industries besides professional football, the bosses exercise a good deal of control over your dress on the job, your hours of coming and going, and even your weight and physical condition.

Most other types of mass entertainment—movies, the theater, music, and particularly the ballet—have their dehumanizing aspects too. Directors and conductors yell at performers, ridicule their performance, and use insults to drive them to greater efforts. Ballet dancers have to follow rigid rules of diet and exercise; they are probably scolded into unified performance more frequently than football players.

It isn't easy to feel much like a human being in the army. It hardly inspired me to have a captain bellow at me when I returned to my outfit from two weeks of "summer activity" at Fort Roberts, because I did not look like a recruiting poster. I had wiped the dust off my combat boots and cleaned myself up. But my hair was long and my boots did not gleam. I had no clean uniform. So the captain blew his stack. Wasn't I ashamed? I wasn't, but I did not argue. If I was going to be ashamed of anything, it was of spending two weeks maintaining the barracks and "taking care" of officers at Fort Roberts, when better men than I were bleeding in Viet Nam.

"Get your hair cut by 11 o'clock!" the good captain bellowed. I did and felt not a damn bit better for it. (Just before the Dallas game, Charley Waller accused me of looking "like a goddam hippy Communist" because I was wearing my baseball cap that made my hair billow out behind.)

Just having someone make money out of exhibiting your muscular efforts is essentially dehumanizing, I suppose. But narcotics and poverty and living in slums and fighting useless wars are the really dehumanizing aspects of our society. Beside them, the degrading elements of professional sports seem trifling.

As for drugs, plenty of guys have used them. There are probably a dozen or so guys with us who will smoke pot from time to time. I am not one of them. But I was once accused by a coach of being a pot-smoker, or at least of having been present at a pot party. He was away off base and I have no idea what evidence he based his charge on.

Amphetamines and the like have been used pretty freely in past years throughout the pro football circuit—just as freely perhaps as they are used by writers, and advertising men, and doctors, and artists, and actors, and musicians. Once or twice since I joined the Chargers I have seen an opposition player popping capsules into his mouth as if they were salted peanuts. Occasionally I have seen an opposing lineman with his eyes bugged out like golf balls, obviously charged up to the point of bursting. But no one on our club has any drugs forced on him. Nor does anyone ever use anything more than the ordinary greenies, which some men get because they want them and have them prescribed. Some guys may receive one in the morning or one just before a game, in accordance with the doctor's advice. They are not for me and not for many of the other guys, who need nothing to stir us to action but the natural additives the glands pump into the blood stream. But I am damned if I see anything so frightening about the controlled use of these stimulants. They are prescribed for all kinds of people who want to lose weight or who need to subject their brains or bodies to sudden unusual demands. I know there would be one hell of a howl—and not just from football players—if doctors were no longer allowed to give them to their patients.

Anyway, in a world where even school kids feel they must drop acid or smoke pot or hash just to fit themselves to cope with the stresses of everyday life, I think there are more serious problems than the consumption of diet pills by professional athletes.

Pro athletes do a hell of a lot more drinking of booze than they do popping of pills and not much is made of it, except by certain coaches. And sometimes the coaches themselves have not been above taking on a load well above their rated capacity. As for me, I am in favor of moderate drinking. I think a drink or two before dinner, a big glass of cold brew after a ball game, and even a few extra drinks on an off day, can untie the knots in a guy's nervous system, still the quivering in his stomach, aid his digestion, unsnarl his disposition, and soothe the aches in his muscles and in his psyche.

Of course no one can be an alcoholic and hold a job for long on a pro football team. Most players are fretful about their physical condition and will check themselves if booze begins to fatten them up or slow them down. There are some players who can consume oversize loads of liquor with no obvious ill effects. Our tough man, Walter Sweeney, an old-fashioned Irishman, can put away double what I can handle. Yet I have never seen him as drunk as I have known myself to be. In fact, Walter Sweeney is one man who practically never has been seen in need of a strong hand to steady him or steer him home.

Despite all the rules and lectures and fines and threats, guys do of course occasionally go overboard. That is usually because booze and broads seem inseparable.

Every city has its body shops and no one has to look through the yellow pages to find them. Sometimes you have to scout a little to locate the place that draws the best supply of unescorted girls. Usually it's a place that is strong on atmosphere and weak on food. But who comes to such places to eat? The best of them have live music at least part of the time, so you can make your play without having everyone nearby checking your technique.

There seems to be a natural affinity between airline stewardesses and pro athletes. Partly because the steward-esses are always in good supply, are far from home, and are unattached, just as the athletes are. But largely it is because the stewardesses can have more fun with an athlete than with, for instance, some post-thirty executive type who is off the reservation for a week. For someone to bounce around with—from bar to bar or even from town to town—a pro athlete, I think, is first choice among the airline girls.

It seems to me that in these encounters the sexes are about as equal as nature or Women's Lib ever intended. You can say, I suppose, that the guy, with his mind centered on screwing, is using the girl as a sex object. But no more than the girl is using the man. And along the way they both manage to have a lot of laughs and take pleasure in each other's company.

I know that oftentimes when a couple of hard-core tailhounds get together, there are not many laughs as each one zeroes in on getting the other one into the hay. But it seems to me that most of the young people, even though they are intent on enjoying each other's bodies, respect each other too, treat each other with consideration, and are content to share as much fun as one night has room for. I don't see that anybody is being taken advantage of, even if the guy picks up the check.

Not many girls who frequent these places are looking for a permanent relationship, any more than the guys are. Both sides want a carefree attitude, no obligations, no holds barred. Both sides want to laugh and drink and listen to music and ultimately land in the hay together, then go their separate ways. Sometimes a friendship develops that is free of obligations and the two get together again whenever their schedules bring them back at the same time.

Unmarried pro athletes usually have money enough to finance an evening like this without strain. But sometimes the girls have been known to kick in a few bucks to make the evening complete. So nobody comes out of it feeling he has been taken or that he must figure out ways of getting an additional return on his investment. And the girls who go in for this life are not looking for a retirement program either. They are out to enjoy their youth, just the way the guys are, without caring when the sun comes up or what it brings with it.

In San Diego, there is not the choice of drinking spots that New York offers. I don't think any city matches New York in its variety of places to keep the evening alive and jumping. If the music or the booze or the company begins to grow stale at one spot you can just hop into a cab for the other side of town where everything starts up fresh again. In San Diego, you have your pick of about half a dozen places: Bully's, Harvey Wallbanger's, the Green Onion, the Hideaway, and one or two more.

If you want female companionship, with the usual fifty-fifty chance of winding up in the hay together, but with at least the assurance that you will have laughs and reasonably intelligent conversation and an attractive face and figure to dote on, you go to Bully's. If you want strictly hard-core girls whose aim is to get to screwing with a minimum of preliminaries, you choose the Hideaway. The others are a little more hit-or-miss.

Professional athletes usually do pretty well at any of these places, although hardly any of us rates instant recognition in public. Indeed you have to put your sunglasses on to identify yourself as a football player, even among the fans in the street.

Lack of national fame probably puts some geographic limits on your scoring opportunities in this game. If you are Joe Namath, you can walk into any body shop on the continent and be certain that a fair supply of lovelies will know you and want to collect your autograph or some such thing. If you are just a San Diego Charger, you do best to enter a strange drinking spot with a crowd of your kind. In most of the hip places, particularly if they are frequented by the local athletes, the regulars all know what ball club is in town, so when a horde of oversize young males surges through the front door, they don't have to introduce themselves as the Chargers. Once in a while there will be a girl who can even call you by name, and when that happens a score is practically assured. However, if you wander in alone, hardly anyone accuses you of being a pro football player and you may have to waste some time exchanging signals.

It is a fact that pro athletes, besides being young and fairly well-heeled, are generally uncomplicated guys who are looking for a whole evening of fun. On that account they undoubtedly look better to the girls who are in the market for the same goods.

We have one conniver on our club who makes it a practice always to gather up the four ugliest jocks on the squad, pile into a cab with them, and take off for the recommended drinking place, confident that when the bitches (a topflight girl, in pro football parlance, is a "fine bitch") make their choice, he will be number one.

Usually the odds favor the visiting team when we are all together in a spot patronized by the locals. The guarantee of no permanent relationship is missing when a girl dates a guy who is going to show up nearly every night. Besides, when a guy carries an air of far-off places he has a special appeal, particularly to the local ladies.

Like any normally delinquent young man, I did my best to win at least Honorable Mention in the sex department and even made a try for election as King of the Over-the-Hill Brigade (the guys who miss bed-check). But in that effort I loused up the play completely.

It happened last year, in Cleveland, just after our game there. The period before the game—a whole week of concentration-camp isolation—was spent in a college dormitory in Wooster, Ohio, where we saved money for the Charger management and learned to look on a bagful of hamburgers from Macdonald's as a form of riotous living.

You can imagine that when we came to Cleveland at last and played our game, the players deployed through Cleveland's bright light area like a troop of sailors off a six-month voyage. I probably knew the name of the place I went to with a few of my mates but I very soon forgot it. It was not, I recall, the "recommended" spot, which was a roadhouse in the suburbs, too far for us to get to and return by plane time. But it was swarming with local lovelies, not all of them escorted, and so it had just the "atmosphere" we were seeking.

I don't have the patience to count over everything that was done or said leading up to my sitting next to one of the sexiest girls in the room and paying for her drinks. None of my brilliant remarks come back to me and hardly any of hers. I do remember that I started out drinking scotch and soda while she drank wine and that we both wound up drinking champagne.

It never occurred to me for a moment as the evening grew deeper and deeper that I was going to finish the night anywhere except snuggled naked in her arms. This prospect seemed more and more imminent, inevitable, and enticing as I plunged deeper into each new bottle of fizz. We sat close, we kissed, we held each other fiercely by the hands, and I felt masterful enough to kick a pathway to the door through a mob of sex-crazed linebackers.

We made the door all right and even made the door to her place, where I arrived panting. And what I got there was a stiff-arm so sudden and final I half expected to hear the whistle blow. So, after a brief drunken protest, I rode glumly back to the hotel, slammed open the door, bringing John Hadl straight up in bed, then suddenly realized I must find the john or disgrace myself.

I turned back in the dark, yanked open the first door, and whacked my face into the wall of the clothes closet. And before I could reorient myself and reel out again to select the right door, my stomach announced it had had enough and it returned—with increment—the entire mess I had crowded into it throughout that glorious evening.

Oh, God! How that closet stank! And how I lay and cursed myself when the sun pried my eyes open next day. For this exploit, instead of receiving the title of King of the Over-the-Hill Gang, I became known as "Three-beer Marty!"

I admit it, there are a number of guys on our squad who can outdo me in this aspect of pro football and I am no longer going to try for the title. Our club assesses a thousand-dollar fine for any aggravated violation of the curfew, and a standard five hundred dollars for missing bed-check. It requires great determination and agility to go out in a strange city, find a willing and attractive sex partner, put her in a receptive mood, board her, and get back before the assistant coach looks in to see if your head is on your pillow. As I explained earlier, this maneuver in pro football circles is now given the technical name of "Bump-and-Run." And just as bump-and-run has become a popular method of pass defense on the field, it has acquired permanent popularity on the motel circuit—not as a defense but, if I can be allowed this one lousy pun, as a means of completing a pass.

What effect this tactic is going to have on the psychic health of the guys and girls who employ it, on the moral fiber of the nation, or on the relative strength of the home team in pro football contests I am not qualified to decide.

It is obvious to me, however, that one of the major fringe benefits of pro football is the willingness of young women to hop into the hay with even a lowly member of the kickoff team or the cab squad. It is not just the Joe Namaths and the other headline heroes who make out wherever they go—it is almost every player who wants to try. This, rather than any haphazard or regular use of artificial stimulants, might deserve the attention of sociologists and reformers. Free sex of this sort is just as habit-forming as the use of amphetamines, far more pervasive, and ten times as much fun. And it thrives, invariably, where alcohol is consumed.

For my part, I can't see anything so damned wicked about it. If both parties are willing and enjoy their sex in hit-and-run fashion, I think that's their concern, so I am not urging the Commissioner to investigate or Congress to pass a law. I just thought I'd mention it. Maybe if there *is* anything wrong about it, it is connected with the whole question of the position of women in our society. And I am not ready to take up that subject.

No matter what you do, however, you are not going to stop pro football players from drinking. If practice is rugged and play is hard, it is impossible to maintain a regular schedule of drinking without having your tongue dragging on the ground, so the best preventive is hard work.

Moral suasion sure as hell is not going to work on a

crowd of fully grown male athletes, many of whom have seen more of the seamy side of life than their employers could even begin to describe. And anyway, moralizing sounds pretty fatuous when it issues from the mouth of some guy who has himself won notoriety as a booze-fighter. Some coaches use fines to keep guys off hard liquor during the training season. But usually, when you are competing for a job on a pro football team, you don't need anyone to warn you not to give the opposition an advantage by tampering with your own physical condition. No full-time drunk, or steady drinker, can stand up long under the strain of a tough two-a-day practice season. The days of the hobo athletes who used to be sobered up on the sidelines before dashing in to carry the ball to victory are now part of the Dark Backward and Abysm of time. Not one of those guys could last a single quarter in a modern pro football game.

4

Offense and Defense

It takes five years, they say, to make a pro quarterback. It takes one year to understand what a hell of a lot there is to learn about the job.

A quarterback, assuming he has all the basic skills (and he would never be a pro without them), has to learn first of all to take charge. It is not in the nature of most guys, even big strong guys who have been made heroes of in school, to wade into the middle of a mob of veterans and not only tell them what to do but make them listen. In the beginning I could not even make all the players shut up in the huddle. Who was I to be giving instructions to some of the greatest players in the game—to Lance Alworth, for instance, who would come into every huddle bubbling with earnest suggestions? Usually his suggestions consisted of assurance that the other side was giving him the "up"—the fly pattern—or the quick-out. Well, Lance's quick-out, which was supposed to see him go four yards downfield and cut straight across, was often a sudden-out, in which he would cut right across the scrimmage line. As for his having the up, he *always* had that, to his way of thinking. He has supreme confidence, great coolness, and the best pair of hands in the business. But I was wasting huddle time trying to hear his suggestions. Eventually I learned to tell him: "Shut up! I'm calling the plays!" From that time on, the other kibitzers were silent too and I was able to take complete charge, as I should have at the start.

After that, it is a matter of reading the defenses and knowing your players. I'll always insist that defense wins

48

pro football games. And the major aspect of the defense
is pass defense. The pros just don't emphasize the running
game the way the colleges do. And you can often detect
when a team is dogging (or blitzing) by the sort of pass
defense they present.

For instance, if the linebacker is playing inside the wide
receiver, this means the weak safety is going to have to
play the wide receiver man to man. And that is not usually
done, unless they are dogging. And so on.

In my first scrimmage against the Rams, I was all
smartened up from my studies and prepared to key (that
is, use an opponent's movements as a key to what the
defense is going to do) the strong safety, Ed Meador. So
I started to call signals, looking over the defense. I looked
at Ed Meador and found him grinning at me. He *knew* I
was trying to read his movements. For some reason this
disconcerted me. Of course, I should have realized that
he *would* know and would not be about to give anything
away. Still, when he made a sudden start off to his left I
very brilliantly tried to complete a pass to his right. And
he moved right in and busted it up. It was the simplest
thing in the world. He had just faked me out. It would
be a while before I learned that I could "look off" a
defender myself, by directing my gaze at the wrong spot
for a while before turning to pick up the primary receiver.

Every club, you learn, has its own way of using even the
standard defenses, so you need to familiarize yourself with
these peculiarities. The National Conference generally
sticks to the good old four-three, which is the easiest of
all to throw against. The American Conference gives you
all sorts of variations and even a few far-out ones like
Hank Stram's three-stack defense (three defenders lined up
one behind the other at crucial points). And of late there
has been much more use of zones, which adds to the
quarterback's problems. Against a deep zone, for instance,
it is useless to try the post pattern, because there will
always be a defender between the receiver and the goal,
and when a receiver breaks to the inside against a deep
zone, he will find double trouble.

It took me more than a little while to learn which players

I could depend on for sound information. Lance's constant assurance that he could "get the up" on some guy was just part of Lance's supreme self-confidence, which helps to make him so damn good, but I could not rely on it. On the other hand, when Gary Garrison says he can do something, he is usually right. He has just as much confidence as Lance, but it does not bubble over. If Gary, on third and ten for instance, tells you "I can beat this guy to the outside," you can be sure he can do just that. If you can get the ball to him then, you are going to have first down and some more.

Not that Lance was always wrong by any means. He was often quick to figure out the weakness of a defender and he could help you immeasurably by his incredible ability to hang on to anything that even touched his fingers. In the Houston game last season, Zeke Moore had been ruining our slant by closing right in on Lance and breaking up the pass. "Try a pump fake on the slant," said Lance, "and I can run right by Moore." So I called the play again, and pumped the ball once toward Lance. Sure enough, Zeke Moore bit on it, closed in on Lance, and Lance sprinted right by him. Then I underthrew the damn ball and it would have been one more incompletion except that Lance slowed down, snagged the ball in his fingertips, and pulled it in. He could hold on to practically anything he could touch. When Lance had a good day the Chargers had a good day. Believe me, I'm going to miss him now that he has gone to Dallas.

Until a quarterback gets to know, not just the possibilities and probabilities of certain defenses, but the idiosyncrasies of his own players, he cannot work effectively. That is one reason why quarterbacks get better and better. Of two guys who may have equal skills, the veteran always has the edge. The veteran, just from knowing all the things that *might* happen, will usually react correctly when something unusual comes up in a game. And veterans also have a way of pulling themselves and a team together to turn defeat into victory. The football players have an expression for this. When a guy like Johnny Unitas, for instance, after two or three futile quarters, finally begins to connect on his passes and call his plays with precision, they will say he is "getting all his shit together." It has taken me a long time to "get all my shit together" and it may be that I still have a long way to go.

There are so many oddities and peculiarities to notice and file away: Does a team habitually collapse its zones? Does this receiver have a tendency to run "bananas"— i.e., gently curving patterns—when a square-out is called for? Which receiver do you choose when you have got two of them on one defender? (The one the defender does *not* choose, of course. But you cannot get in a rut about receivers and *always* favor one over the other.)

Most of all, you get to know your players, and what they are capable of. You look for holes, even when a play goes bad. Could it have worked if sent in a different direction? There is a running back on our club named Brad Hubbert who has got himself persuaded that he cannot run to his left. I am convinced that this is all psychological. But you still have to reckon with it, because he is convinced that there is better blocking to his right. So I try always to oblige—by sending him to his right or straight up the middle. Otherwise I let him block for Dickie Post.

Dickie likes to carry the ball and loves to play but he grows irritated at constant criticism of his failure to block. Dickie *does* block but he is so small the defensive men just shed him.

Sometimes I wish I could develop Dickie's cool attitude toward the game. He plays hard, with every ounce of his strength, yet I never saw him tensed up or jittery between times. I can recall one game in which Dickie sat all alone at one end of the bench, with a blanket over his head, like an abandoned Indian, not seeming to hear or see anything that went on around him. Suddenly Charley Waller called to him to warm up. Dickie shed his blanket, stood up, bent over once and touched his toes, and sat right down in his previous pose. Yet when the coach sent him in, he charged out like a Comanche and threw himself right into the crush. Soon afterward, he took off with the ball and was belted out of bounds near our bench, the blow sending him several yards outside the boundary stripe, where he lay on the grass, obviously shaken.

He looked up at Waller: "Do you really want me to go *back* in there?" he said. Then he hopped up and trotted into the huddle.

Later in the same game, another play brought Dickie over the sidelines, somewhat shaken and completely winded. I think he exaggerated his panting a bit as he looked up in pretended envy at the rest of us, all comfortably snuggled in our blankets and watching the play. "Boy," said Dickie, "are you guys lucky you don't have to get into *this!* They're *hitting!*"

Dickie really isn't little by ordinary standards because he must weigh about 190. But he is not tall and he is outweighed fifty and sixty pounds by most of the men he runs into. If anybody could feel exploited, put upon, and brutalized, you'd think it might be Dickie. But he loves the game and enjoys life as much as any man in the league. More than most. Dickie operates a clothing shop that features mod clothes and most of the players, including me, buy clothing there. Dickie himself, on his motorcycle, with his hair flowing out behind like one of General Custer's scouts, is "mod" from top to toe. If the game has dehumanized Dickie in the least, he has managed to keep it concealed.

Observation, getting to know all my teammates' idiosyncrasies—these have kept me busier than I thought I would ever be. Starting out in a state where I hardly knew how to address some of my older teammates, I gradually got so I could almost read their minds. Today I can walk into a barroom and sit down with five of my mates and order drinks for everybody without asking any of them their preferences. I know what they like to drink as well as I know which way they like to run.

Of course you can get into trouble by being superconfident, as I did at Harvey Wallbanger's one day. I ordered drinks for everybody at my table—my two teammates and two girls—and told the man what everybody else (six more guys) wanted too. What I did not realize was that the man expected me to *pay* for all ten drinks I named. I had just money enough for one round for *us*. Well, a quarter-back learns by trial and error.

Another man I have learned to rely on is center Sam Gruneisen, who is even more of a leader of our offensive linemen than the line coach is. Sam, with his flaming red hair, his eager, boyish look (he is thirty but looks twenty-one) and his complete involvement in the play, is just naturally the man the other guys follow. And when he tells me that on second down the defense has been stunting to the wide side and that he can kill them with a trap back to the weak side, I don't have to ask him how he knows. I just call the play and it goes.

Sam is always right about whatever he is doing. There never was an athlete who took sports more seriously. When he is not involved in football he is over his ears in golf, working at that as though the fate of the world hung on every stroke. Sam is strictly a family man and has no time for what the rest of the team considers "relaxation." He brings his kids to Saturday morning practice, without fail, so they can study Daddy's ways and be wise.

I suppose you could argue that a man has to be partly nuts to take any sport as seriously as Sam takes them all. I know I could not ever be as grim about a golf game as Sam is, or even about football or rugby, the two games I love most. But if a man intends to be good at something, he has to be serious about it.

There is an odd contradiction here too: You don't enjoy a game properly unless you play it well. And you don't play it well unless you take it seriously, at least while you are involved in it. I have noticed that some of the playboy types and even the laughing boys are grim as gunmen when the ball is in play. And I have also observed that some fellows will clown it up all over the field as a means of excusing their own inability to complete a play.

Anyway, why not be serious about what you do? I find some sales conferences—where guys are grim as death about promoting some phony tonic that is supposed to double a man's sex appeal—far more comic than being grim about a game, where the guy with the most ability and determination can win lifetime success, regardless of where he came from or what color he is.

I did discover, however, that it is possible to concentrate too long and hard. It took me two years to find out that I actually played better football if, instead of using all my spare time studying films and fretting over mistakes, I forgot the game in the evening and had fun.

Pro football differs from college football not only in the skills and size of the performers but in mental attitude. Among the pros you never find that pervasive gung-ho feeling that is common to college clubs before a crucial game. The pros generally approach a game in a business-like manner and are no more likely to gather to whoop up their fighting spirit before a game than a team of doctors would meet to listen to a "Let's go get 'em" speech from the head surgeon before a big operation.

But a rookie quarterback is something else. When I first got word that I was actually going to play in a game—the exhibition game in my rookie year against New Orleans— I generated as much inner tension as I ever had before a college game. Everyone else, even coach Gilman, was wholly relaxed. It was not really a game to them, just an advanced form of practice in which the coach could try out some plays and see what they looked like against real opposition. But I never relaxed. I could feel myself building up to "readiness" just as if this were the big game of the year.

In the locker room before the game there was not a word of the inspirational muck that college coaches like to serve up. John Hadl and I simply sat and went over the game plan together, with him telling me which plays he thought might work under certain circumstances and which plays he had doubts about. Just the same, I could feel myself trembling inwardly.

I was slated to go in at the opening of the second quarter. As I always do, I imagined the game situation I would want to find when I went in—perhaps a fumble that would give us the ball at about our own 20-yard line— some place that called for a long bomb. I would connect of course and score—and . . . I could feel that tingle on my scalp as the cheers poured down on me.

My warm-up was good, crisp moves, on-target passes. But I could feel that little hand clutching at my stomach now and then and taking my breath away, something I had not felt since I first started to play varsity football at Columbia. I wanted, not just to move the team, but to make a SPLASH that could be heard all over San Diego.

My job in the first quarter was to wear the headset that transmitted all the instant wisdom from the assistant coach in the pressbox. As I digested and passed along the word from above, I tried to put out of my mind the plays that had not been working and to figure out some sort of rhythmic pattern of the Saints' defensive moves in the various situations. All the while, of course, my heart rhythm remained stepped up, for I was watching the clock move closer and closer to the moment when I would make my debut as a pro.

The quarter ended. I swallowed to wet my dry throat and looked at Sid Gilman, but Sid, inasmuch as neither team had done anything offensively that was worth noting, decided to keep John in the game for another series of downs. So I waited and sweated a little longer.

We punted. The Saints were stalled. Then their punter dropped one on our three-yard line. What a spot! And sure enough, this was the very spot Sid chose for my entry. With the adrenalin pouring into my veins at a rate of about two ounces a second, I trotted, head high, out to the huddle. The moment I stepped on the field the PA man announced my presence. There was a sudden and what seemed to me a prolonged roar from the big crowd—the loudest and longest cheer I had ever received. I tried to keep from grinning with excitement.

It had been my dream that we would be in a position where I could fire the bomb at once and swell those cheers to three times their volume. But how the hell could I throw a bomb from the three-yard line? I ran two running plays to gain a little elbow room, then tried a screen pass that fell incomplete. Now, instead of being glad and excited, I was completely pissed off—not at anyone or anything, but at Fate—or whatever it was that enabled the Saints' punter to put the ball within one stride of our goal line. Now I withdrew to the sidelines and waited until we got the ball back.

On the second try, Fate lined up *with* me. We had the ball on our own 20—just the spot for that killer pass for the score, the pass my yearning arm had been ready for since Tuesday last.

The play I called was known as PP 35 Z Up—the PP indicating a play-action pass, the 35 indicating who was to put on the action and where, and the rest telling that Gary Garrison was to take off on the fly. Even though I must be the one to say it, I put on a good, convincing fake. I hid the ball successfully (I think) against my belly, fell back the proper distance, turned, read the defense, found Gary just running by his man, and then unleashed what I felt was a sure strike.

The roar of the crowd went up, up, up—oooOOOO-OOOH!—then as the ball just slid off Garrison's very fingertips, it faded to an AAAAaaaaaaah! My own spirits performed the same figure—up, up, UP, and then DO-oooown with a dismal plop. I had simply underestimated the amount of adrenalin that was firing up my furnaces and had thrown the damn ball too far.

After that, I settled to playing routine football. We made a couple of first downs, but we did not score, and I went to the sidelines annoyed at myself, yet somehow satisfied too. I had moved the club some. I had not been involved in any disaster. And when I left the field after that series of downs, the crowd once more cheered me—not so long this time, but heartily and approvingly. So, in the words of John Hadl, I left the field a happy cowboy.

What pleased me most, after I had shed the disappointment of not bombing the Saints off the field with one mighty sweep of my arm, was my success at reading the defenses. That was the fruit of my hours and hours of movie-going—the movies of course being action pictures of enemy football clubs. Quarterbacks have to study defensive men the way a champion base-stealer studies the moves of pitchers. You have to read at a glance what sort of pass

coverage your receivers are going to run into and you
should be able to detect the "dog" in advance so you can
take advantage of it by passing into the deserted areas.

The most elementary coverage is what we call "cover
two," in which the secondary covers the potential receivers
man to man—the strong cornerback covering the flanker,
the strong safety lining up on the tight end, the weak-side
cornerback taking the split end man to man, and the weak
safety playing centerfield, over the ball, watching the
quarterback's eyes for the give-away sign and helping out
on the inside as he is needed.

But the defense may line up like this and still go into a
zone defense, with varying rotations. So you watch the
strong safety for the tip-off. (Of course you have been
studying his behavior all week in the films, or you certainly
will be fooled by him.)

Is the strong safety playing a little deeper than ordinary,
to the outside of the tight end? Then he is probably not
covering the tight end man to man but is preparing to
"rotate" in a zone formation, in which he is responsible
for the deep zone. Because he will have a long way to go
to get into position, he is cheating just a bit in the direction
of his coverage. This is what we call the "cloud" rotation
and the coverage is called "cover three." From the same
coverage it may be possible to detect a "sky" rotation, in
which the strong-side linebacker drops back and the strong
safety moves over laterally into the area the strong-side
linebacker just abandoned.

"Cover One" is a dog—in which the linebackers will be
blasting in to nail the quarterback. In this formation, the
weak-side safety will move in close, off the ball a little, to
cover the halfback man to man.

There are some clubs that use a combination zone and
man-to-man coverage, and you have to learn to recognize
those too. For instance, there is "cover five," in which each
cornerback is responsible for the receiver on his end, while
the two safeties and the strong linebacker cover, respective-
ly, the tight end and the strong-side backs. The weak-
side safety, in this coverage, is not free to roam centerfield.
So he plays up rather tight and edges a shade over toward

the tight end, whom he must cover if the tight end "releases," or breaks loose, *inside* the strong linebacker.

If, in this form of coverage, the offensive back on the strong side (the "strong" side is where flanker and tight end play) goes outside the strong-side linebacker and upfield, then the strong safety must cover him deep. But the strong-side linebacker will "ride him up" to the safety's area. Conversely, if the tight end goes outside, on an "out" or "corner" pattern, the strong safety must pick *him* up while the weak safety takes the offensive back who goes inside. The strong-side linebacker will take the man going outside as far as the deep zone, where the strong safety will take over.

And just to make this more confusing, there is a further variation if the tight end moves straight out into the flat. In that instance, he must be covered by the strong-side linebacker, while the strong safety, with no one coming into his zone, is freed to help out where needed. The weak safety in this variation must take the halfback man to man.

So the key to it is still the strong safety. Is he tight and shaded toward the tight end? Or it is possible to read this from the position of the weak cornerback, who will be lined up deeper than ordinary and somewhat to the inside, to take away the post pattern.

The point of all the "reading," of course, is to help you know where the open places will be, or where you will have a backfield man working against a linebacker—who is usually slower. When a zone defense is being used, there will be "seams"—spots where the zones overlap and where coverage may be handed over from one man to another, with a consequent momentary lapse of coverage.

A quarterback cannot afford the time to think these things out. In the few seconds he takes to drop back and set up in his passing position he must notice and react instinctively to what he sees, the way a man fielding a baseball reacts instinctively to its bounce. How deep-rooted this instinct can become was illustrated to me when I once managed to pick up the dog, call an audible against it at the line, and pass for a score—all while I was effectively "unconscious."

This happened in the Houston game at the Astrodome in my rookie year. It was third down and ten on the Houston 27 when I observed that the weak safety, in "cover one," was playing tight. In addition (my teammates told me afterward) the linebackers were revving up for the blitz. I promptly called an audible—one of the approved plays on our "audible list" for this game. It was what we know as a Z post—meaning that "Z", the flanker back, runs toward the goal post to take the pass downfield. Sure enough, the defense dogged, Gary broke loose all alone at the goal line, and I put the ball right in his hands.

Afterward, when I was being congratulated on my shrewdness in calling that audible that I could not remember, I took real satisfaction in it. But at half time, when Houston was leading 17 to 7, I could recall none of the action except their field goal.

They had scored quickly from our 30 and after the kickoff I had trotted in, cool and confident, loping easily along, almost tasting the excitement that filled my veins. We moved quickly to a first down and then the coach sent in the "bomb" we had planned for this game—a "can't-miss" play that called for me to bootleg off a fake end sweep and hit Lance Alworth on a deep post.

I faked successfully and bootlegged the ball out, looking casually downfield for Lance. Ahead of me trotted Bill Lenkaitis, who was to have blocked out the linebacker. But the linebacker had dogged and, along with most of the defense, had followed the apparent flow of the play.

Suddenly I saw an opening before me—only safety man George Webster to keep me from a fifteen-yard gain. And I had a blocker who was certain to clear Webster out. I faked a move to the outside and cut in behind Bill. But all Bill did was fall to the ground in Webster's vicinity. Then Webster hit me about ankle high and sent me into orbit. I actually made a complete somersault in the air. (My mother, watching it on TV, said the announcer laughed during the instant replay and commented: "That's why they pay quarterbacks to stand back and *throw*.") Down I came, all 220 pounds, upon the goddamn Astroturf with a thundering impact. My head whacked hard against the surface.

The Astroturf being about as resilient as the floor of a basketball court, I saw the whole sky explode before my eyes. I got up and *thought* I felt fine, but the coach sent John in to relieve me and I went to the sidelines snarling to myself. But the coach assured me I might get back in if I really felt "all together." The trainer asked me a row of questions and apparently I gave all the right answers for very soon afterward I trotted back in to take charge once more. What I did after that I knew only from watching the films. (The coach kept telling me, as I made that try for a fifteen-yard gain: "For no reason! No *reason!*" How right he was!)

Two downs after I returned, handicapped by a slowdown in my reactions, I threw a really *ridiculous* interception. They took the ball in and made the score 10 to 0. (It was still 3 to 0 in my consciousness.)

But our defense held them pretty well after that and my "great audible" came when we had marched to their 27. Soon after that, however, I again threw too soon and too short—and again they grabbed the ball and took it in to make it 17 to 7.

I was disappointed when I heard John was going to start the second half. But I could hardly protest, for I could not recall *anything* I had done, good or bad. I just stood there wondering how the hell the score, which had just been 3 to 0, could have turned into 17 to 7. My reactions, slowed down as they were, were grained deep into my skull by hours of study and practice and at least in that one instance, had been correct. And if I had had my bell rung *before* I tried that no-reason run, I might have thrown to Lance for a touchdown. At least I'd not have gone in for any extraneous thinking. But we did win 21–17.

If only *all* my reactions could have been that automatic! There were many other opportunities that year and the next for me to exhibit my lightning reflexes, and the lightning sometimes flickered out.

The game that I may remember longest was the game

against the New York Giants, to open my sophomore year as a pro. In it I did some things I would just as soon forget, and also some things my grandchildren will probably grow tired of hearing about.

I prepared for the game by lying awake most of the night, two nights before. I watched movies of the Giants over and over again, trying to decide if it was just poor photography, or if the Giants were really that bad. Watching the films, and in waking dreams afterward, I must have played the whole game through at least ten times, figuring out new ways to beat them. Here was my favorite scenario: The Giants win the toss and receive. Then they fumble near our 20-yard line (they had done that before) and I go in and score with a play-pass, a bootleg, and a long bomb to Gary Garrison. And after that I could just follow the game plan, with no need to go in for desperation passes to catch up.

Was I getting overconfident? I tried to make myself think that the Giants were *not* all that bad. They might— and this is what I wanted least—go ahead and score three times and leave me with my tongue out, trying all night to catch up. I forced myself to think hard about what I might have to do and I told myself again and again not to grow too confident.

I had to remember not to use any too-fancy audibles if Pettis Farrar played. Pettis was kind of a free-wheeling guy who has a hard time remembering any audibles except the ones in which he carries the ball. And I *had* to tell myself that the Giants *did* have a defense. (But the films didn't show it, my other self recalled. The Giants had no stars in that defensive backfield. Well, maybe Spider Lockhart. But would you call him a star?)

The night before the game I took a sleeping pill. It did not help me much. In the morning (the game was to be played in San Diego on Sunday night) I lay in bed a little longer than usual and my mates, walking through the room, pretended to look on this as a sign that I was taking victory for granted. Lying in bed for God's sake instead of hopping out and getting my motors revved up for the biggest day of my life. (It had to be a big day for me, starting a game against my "home" team, and going on national TV, with all my friends and relatives in New York watching.) But I was chewing at myself for petty matters. Janie, my girl friend, had promised to come get some of my clothes and send them to be cleaned, and to leave a note telling when she would be back. She had gone to the races with her father and had forgotten. No note! No clean clothes! Well, I heaved myself out of bed finally and was greeted by a jeering chorus: "Well, for Christ's sake! It's about time you got up and faced it! Were you hoping to sleep through the game?"

I wouldn't say I was tense. But I felt the need for a beer or two to help relax before driving down to the city. There were aspects of my practice that had not pleased me. I had been hitting my receivers all right but I had been throwing "ducks" (wobbly passes) all week. Still I knew that, once in the game, I would be concentrating so on defenses that my passes would automatically start to spiral. It was when I tried to *think* about throwing them properly that I started tossing ducks, and had the guys on the sidelines asking for shotguns to shoot the mallards down.

So I got to the field feeling reasonably cool, with nothing really fretting me but not having any clean clothes for afterward, and my fear of overconfidence. Well, my overconfidence ebbed away very quickly. There was no fumble by the Giants and no mighty TD pass for me. Instead I pulled the goddamndest rock of my life and gave the Giants a head start—just from letting my mind wander. What the *hell* had I been thinking of? I called a pitch-out to the left on a play that only went to the right. We had no version of this play to the left. But when I had the ball in my hands, I turned, all coolness and confidence, and pitched it out *perfectly* to the left, where there was nothing to receive it but the vacant sod. I broke desperately after the ball but I was too late. The Giants recovered it and within seconds they had a touchdown.

When I went to the sideline, Charley Waller was really pissed. "What are you doing, choking up on me?" he shouted. Now I don't mind his finding fault. I had already found fault with my own stupidity. But I did not care for his yelling at me in front of the squad. Choking up! After a whole season as a pro, I should be choking up? I simply could not restrain my anger.

"Oh, for Christ's sake, Charley," I started. . . . But then I took hold of myself and sat down. John Hadl, taking it all in, grinned at me, to indicate that he knew what *that* kind of crap was like.

Later, Charley came to me to ask how I felt and when I growled that I felt fine he laughed and said he had just said that to me to get me into a fighting mood. Oh balls, I thought, but I said nothing. And after letting John run a few plays, he put me back into the game. I had one more bad moment after that, when I found myself trapped behind our goal line with the ball in my hands. Unable to get away from the tacklers, I "fumbled" the ball, saw it roll out over the goal line, and fell on it. The referee looked at me with a slightly quizzical expression. "That was quick thinking," he muttered. *"If* you did it on purpose." Of course that's what he didn't know, and he had to give us the benefit of the doubt and let us keep the ball.

It turned out to be a good game, in which I actually got loose on a scramble for a long run, and when it was over, and we had won, I was so charged up I stood and passed the ball back and forth with a friend in the parking lot. It was past midnight and I could have gone another quarter. A car rolled slowly by and a little boy looked out at me.

"Hey, Marty!" he yelled. "The game is over!"

But the point I wanted to make is that it takes more than one season's experience to give you the sort of training needed to make *all* your moves instinctive. In the Green Bay game I could have used a little more instinct too. It was at one of the high points of my brief career, when I had come in and got the club moving after John Hadl had been stalled. It was right after I had engineered a touchdown, with a play-call of my own that overruled the coach's.

Charley sent word to run off tackle but I called time
and told him we could do better sending the fullback
through the four hole, where I had seen a big gap. He
agreed and we scored easily. Then I had to hold on to
the lead. I could have too, if I had simply held on to the
ball at the right time. But, like most quarterbacks who
lack long experience, I was still reluctant to eat the ball
when there seemed a chance to complete a pass.

I had led the club to two touchdowns and had a one-
point lead, which hardly gave me room to relax. Still, we
had scored fourteen points in six snaps of the ball and
my confidence was high. We were expecting the Packers
to dog on the first play of that particular series but they
did not.

I tried a toss and lost a couple of yards. So I called
play 62—a pass play that was supposed to see the tight
end hook right off the line. But he did not hook when he
should have and Ray Nitschke had time to move over in
front of him.

If I had not felt so damn confident I probably would
never have let the pass go. But I knew that with a completion we might be off to an eight-point lead and I could
not resist that chance for a third touchdown in less than
ten snaps. I pumped the ball once, to give my tight end
time to get over where he should be, then I just floated
the ball to him over Nitschke's head.

The ball rode clear of Nitschke all right. But I had
forgotten what a demon Willie Wood could be. That man
can shift direction quicker than a squirrel. One moment he
was going away from the play and the next he was right
there behind Nitschke to pick off that floating football
as if it had been put up there just for him. That blew the
game. And it also blew my self-esteem. Next time, goddamn it, I told myself, hold *on* to the ball.

Afterward I heard that some of the TV geniuses had
found fault with the play-call suggesting that only a numb-
skull could have called a play where interception was so
easy. But the play-call, I still maintain, was the right one.
If the end had hooked on time, there would have been a
long long gain and the guys in the broadcast booth would

have been sounding off about my brilliance. It was not my first thought that went wrong, it was my second thought —my failure to respond to my instincts. I *knew* the end had hooked too late and I should have taken the loss right then.

"Think of it this way," John Hadl told me afterward. "While you were in there, you beat them, 14 to 3."

John had a way of cheering me that no coach has ever matched. He had been over a rough road and he often warned me not to chew my own ass out the way he had. Don't take criticism seriously, he said. Forget your errors and close your ears to the boos. "They gave me an ulcer," he said. "I accepted the blame for everything."

It is true that a quarterback has a habit of blaming himself—and being blamed—for all the mistakes of his mates. He even has to take the blame deliberately sometimes, to keep a receiver's spirits up. But he has to learn, as a baseball pitcher does, to keep looking ahead and to forget the errors and the mistakes—and the home runs— that are already on the board. It is for helping me to learn this lesson that I am most grateful to John Hadl. I know I cannot do anything about missed assignments and faulty patterns and slippery spots on the turf; I practice telling myself that they all even up in the long run. Once in a while I let my neck grow red at an official. I even, like every other player, occasionally curse out the officials to their faces, to get rid of my own frustrations.

Sid Gilman helped me acquire another quality a quarterback cannot do without—poise on the field of battle. Early in my rookie year I found myself occasionally putting on an act of frustration and dismay at my own stupidities— most of which resulted from my wanting so desperately to look good. I would sometimes see my passes wobble end over end, or fall ten yards short, or sail off into the yonder. Then I would exhibit open disgust and anger at myself. I suppose if there had been a water cooler handy, I'd have punched it. But Sid pulled me up sharp one morning.

"*Never* show your feelings that way!" he warned me. "A quarterback is supposed to *lead!*"

He did not have to tell me that twice. Practically from
the moment he said it, I changed my ways. It was just
a matter of seeing myself as I must have looked to everyone else. That very afternoon I went out to practice with
a "hell-with-it" attitude toward my own mistakes; for the
first time in several days I threw not a single duck and
hit my receivers consistently.

Every quarterback naturally develops his own favorite
methods and pet plays. His favorite opposition too. My
own favorite team to play against was the Oakland Raiders,
because they could be depended on to use the exact same
defense play after play. Against the Raiders you never
had to bother trying to read the defenses. You just knew
it would be straight 4–3 with man-to-man coverage. That
is the easiest to deal with and the one I would have
preferred to face every Sunday. The trouble was of course
that the Raiders had one hell of an offense, so that you
never could tell yourself two or three touchdowns were
enough. It's always "Let's try for one more" against that
club, because they can come from behind and grab you
in less time than any other team I know. The Big Play
is their specialty.

The toughest defense to figure out was the Cincinnati
Bengals. You could not count on them to repeat themselves at any time. There is never anything stereotyped
about that club, this being a reflection I suppose of Coach
Paul Brown's busy mind. They have four or five different
coverages and there is no telling which they may select
under any given circumstance.

My favorite plays are several. One running play that
I like, because it is so soundly planned and offers such a
high chance of success, is designed to make four or five
yards. It is called "26 bob tray O." The 26 indicates that
it is of the "20" series and that the ball will be carried
through the six hole, between right guard and tackle. The
"bob" (short for back on blocker) means that the outside
back is to take the linebacker nose to nose—put his head
right in the guy's numbers and run over him. The "tray"
is a code to indicate the line-blocking, which includes
double-teaming of the defensive end by the right end and

tackle. The "O" means that the offside guard (the guard away from where the play is being run) is to pull out and lead the play through the hole.

I like this basic play because it is just a good solid down-and-dirty play designed to concentrate the offensive strength at the point of attack. The double-team blocking gives a special advantage. The back does not have too far to run to reach the hole. The pulling guard makes it almost certain the runner will get through, so you have a fine chance of picking up four to five yards on this.

As for passing plays, I lean to the play-action pass. Actually I probably get the most fun out of off-the-wall, gadget plays. But a good basic pass play I feel I can depend on is one that I use when we have the ball on the hash-mark. Then I will put the strength of the formation against the sideline, fake a running play to the wide side, and throw a post pattern to the flanker.

What I like about this play is that it gives the weak or free safety extra ground to cover, and cuts down on his chances of getting to the point of reception on time.

Some clubs, like Green Bay, make no effort to keep the defense guessing, and just count on execution to bring yardage, even if the defense knows exactly what to expect. But I like to spring surprises. Because I enjoy carrying the ball, I will occasionally call an end sweep and not even tell my own club I plan to keep the ball and bootleg it in the direction opposite to the flow of the play. It is a special satisfaction to see a play like that pull the entire defense off in the direction of the fake, while I hotfoot it downfield with the football.

In general, I prefer the plays in which the percentages are on my side. That is one reason why I favor having the quarterback call the plays. He knows what he can do best and will lean to the plays in which he has confidence. Coaches, on the other hand, are inclined to base their play choice on whatever the other side may be "giving us"— that is, on whatever play looks as if it might work against this particular defense.

For instance, they may decide after study of the game films or on the basis of reports from upstairs, that we can

run turn-in patterns against a certain club. But my own
preference, against any club, is for the "out" patterns, the
come-backs, the quick-outs, whatever moves the receiver
away from the concentration of coverage. It just stands
to reason that, when you pass into the area where there
is the greatest concentration of defenders, the percentages
are against you. On turn-ins I just do not have the confidence that I have on the other patterns.

Of course, it gives a quarterback an extra charge to
come up with the solution of a tough problem, so there
is additional reason for wanting to make the call yourself.
If, for instance, you detect the safety blitz (from having
observed the give-away signs in the game films) and you
call the proper audible to take advantage of the fact that
the free safety has vacated his territory, you find an un-
matched thrill in completing the pass for a long gain. We
have an audible, number 46, a tight-end post, that is
designed to deal with the safety blitz. By sending the right
end on a post pattern, with only the wide receiver to run
a complementary pattern on the other side, you keep more
men in the backfield to protect you, giving yourself extra
time to get your pass off, and you put the receiver right
into the spot the safety has abandoned.

There is also special pleasure in pulling yourself out of
a tight spot. If I have gotten myself behind the eight ball
by overthrowing the receiver or failing to connect in some
other way, I dislike having the coach come to my rescue
with a play of his own choice. I recall the time when I
put myself in a deep hole in a game against the Bears by
tossing two incompletions in a row. The play I first called
was one I like—a cross-over pattern to Lance. In this
play the receiver goes six or seven yards downfield and
then "builds a staircase" by running two or three steps
across, then up, across and then up again, until he has
gotten free. (Of course Lance, as I pointed out earlier,
had his own special way of running this pattern and sometimes took right off across the landscape before he had
gone two yards downfield.)

The play is a fake draw into the line, designed to pull
the defense in to stop the run. The first time I tried this,

on first down, the Bears fell for the draw and Lance broke
free immediately. But I underthrew the ball so that not
even Lance, with his weasel-like ability to reverse himself
and fling his body after the ball, could make the completion. So I called the same play again. This time the Bears
must have decided that I was *surely* going for the draw
and they once more left Lance open. This time I threw
the ball high and too far behind him. Now it was third
down and the Bears were certainly familiar enough with
the play to recognize the moves immediately. So I decided
to try it on the other side, to Gary Garrison.

The advantage this time was that the draw really was
in order, so Gary broke away quickly. And I was concentrating harder than before, determined to hit my target.
Gary took the ball in stride and we made a 25-yard gain.

As I said, however, the gadget plays are the ones I take
special pleasure in. These off-the-wall schemes are those
we use to give the team a lift, say after two punt exchanges
have left both sides stagnated. They are not practiced often
and do not possess especially sound design, but they are
exciting to watch and fun to perform.

A typical play of this sort would be called in the huddle
in this fashion: "Fake 28 bob odd O. Z reverse. Throw
back to quarterback. Pass. X jog and up. On two."

The whole design of the play is described in that code.
It is a fake end sweep to the right (the 8 hole). There is
a nose-to-nose block on the linebacker. Both guards (on-
side and offside—odd and O) pull to lead the fake sweep.
The running back hands off to the flanker (Z) and he
pitches the ball back to the quarterback. The split end
(X) meanwhile has started downfield at a jog, perhaps
pretending to have pulled a hamstring or hurt his ankle.
Then he takes off at top speed on the "up" pattern and
the quarterback heaves the ball to him far downfield.

This play can be a killer and everyone gets a wallop out
of it when it works. I think what appeals to me is all the
acting and fakery connected with it. When it is runs properly
it looks exactly like a classic end sweep. Then it becomes
a reverse. Finally it's a pass, with the split end pulling a
bit of acting on his own part. Lance would even go so

far as to fall on his face sometimes to make it seem as if he was out of the play.

Fran Tarkenton of the Giants likes plays of this sort too and he has a great sense of when to toss one in—just when the enemy least expects it.

Learning the offensive plays and developing the skill to run them are two different jobs. A quarterback has to perfect his own technique before he can run any play with confidence. And he particularly needs to learn the idiosyncrasies of his own players, especially the ball carriers and receivers. One of the big jobs is getting himself programmed to drop back the proper distance. Every coach has his own idea of how far back a quarterback should set up and it takes long steady drill to make it a habit to drop back exactly the same distance each time and to do it automatically.

Plays will go wrong sometimes because you do not realize that your pulling guard has got one foot a little deeper into the backfield than is usual for other guards. Then just as you start to hand off, the guard may run into your arm and knock the ball loose. Next time you'll remember to give him room. And pretty soon you'll automatically allow for that extra depth. But these are not things you learn off a blackboard or from having them explained to you. Constant game experience is necessary to turn a college quarterback into a pro. That is one reason why a quarterback, like me, grows restless from being kept too long on the sidelines.

From looking back over my own adjustment period I have concluded that a quarterback—or a baseball pitcher, or for that matter any athlete on whom major plays pivot— has to develop a sort of insulation that keeps him from looking behind him (in time, that is) or from fretting over what might happen to bring disaster around his ears. Likewise a receiver has to learn not to "hear footsteps"— to concentrate so fiercely on the job of catching and holding the ball that all other sound and action, for the crucial few seconds, is closed right out of his mind. I think many rookies suffer from letting their imaginations run free —that is, imagining or trying to put into words what *might* happen—when they should be acting loosely and instinctively.

Sometimes you do hear a coach warn a baseball or football player not to *think*. He does not mean the player should be a robot or a moron, but that he should focus 100 percent on the job in hand and trust to his training and his instincts. "Thinking"—i.e., considering the possibility of doing something wrong, or of getting hurt, or of getting bawled out by the coach or the manager—can cause you to hesitate, to hold back, to look away, to cringe, to get off balance. And it can even get you badly hurt. Too much concern with trying to remember everything you have been told can also break your coordination and louse up your performance.

The injury I suffered in New Orleans came as the result of indecision—an indecision I will never repeat. When I came face to face with the defensive man I had the choice of running right over him or trying to slip away to the safety of the sidelines. I remembered that Sid Gilman had always warned the quarterbacks to run only until they met opposition, and then to go for the sidelines, or hit the turf. I hesitated for a split second while I recalled that advice. And while I hesitated I was hit. Next time I'll run the guy right down.

When teammates and coaches urge a player to "stay loose" they are not suggesting that he be half-hearted or careless in his play. They are warning him against tying himself into mental knots by trying to imagine all the dire possibilities.

I think a guy walking a tight-rope is bound to lose his balance when he starts to think about what might happen. Anyone knows that there is no trick to walking along a plank that is two feet wide without stepping off it. But put that plank up 30 stories high and most people will freeze at the possibilities. The pro athlete has to own the ability to blot such possibilities right out of his mind.

Football players set out to "sting" their opponents, not to break their bones but to try to get them to "thinking" —and consequently cringing and hesitating at the next snap of the ball. When some college hero appears on a

pro kickoff squad for the first time, he can be sure his
opponents are going to try to make sure he does not want
to come back. It is part of the game to try to get the other
guy to thinking about getting hurt instead of thinking about
doing his job.

Ball carriers and linemen have to think, in that they
have to plan ways of getting around opponents, of faking
the enemy into a false move, of forcing a man to use his
own weight against himself, as a backfield man may do
against a heavier lineman in pass protection. But this is
thinking that, if a man practices and plays and studies long
enough and hard enough, does not require words. It
translates instantly into muscular action.

A quarterback has to think double. He has to know
the potentials of all his ball carriers (will he run to his
right?) and the habits of all his receivers (will he "quick-
out" right off the line?). He also has to read the moves
and positions of the enemy and know instantly what they
mean (sometimes he just *thinks* he knows, but he has no
time for working it all out on paper).

To learn to do all that thinking in such a way that it
translates itself into action in fractions of seconds, a
quarterback has to get, not just hours and days, or even
weeks of study and drill and game action behind him, but
years. That is why you don't see college All-Americans
turning instantly into full-blown pros. Even great quarterbacks like Greg Cook, who was forced by shortage of
manpower to take over as first-string quarterback at
Cincinnati, will commit all sorts of rocks, along with his
great passes and play-calls. I think if you go over Cook's
record for his first year you will find it full of hair-
raising mistakes, of the sort I used to think only I could
make. And Cook had the advantage of having his plays sent
in by Paul Brown, who may be the one real genius pro
football has ever produced.

This is why I am a bug about good practice. I want to
develop an instinct for doing things right and I know you
develop instinct only by doing things the right way over
and over and over again. I always admired Y. A. Tittle,
whom I saw only briefly in action (on TV) but have read

a great deal about. Tittle was a man who, they say, wanted to perform perfectly in practice as well as in the game. He believed, along with George Allen, that sloppy practice makes for sloppy play. And that is part of my religion too. I want to get myself to the point where I never have to give a thought to what might happen if things go wrong, where I just *naturally* do things right and can center all my mind on the instant job.

I don't want plays sent in to me, although I know that the coach, being ultimately responsible for victory, has the right to send them. A great part of the fun of football is working out your own ways of moving the team against opposition, noticing weak spots in the defense and calling plays to take advantage, or detecting some give-away move and calling an audible to outwit the other side. I recognize that the aim of pro football is not to provide fun for the quarterback. But when the game stops being fun, I know I'll be looking for a better way to make a living.

5

Sportswriters, and Other Afflictions

A short time ago, when I was home, I read a column in the *New York Daily News*. In it Dick Young, a writer I used to read regularly, allowed that John Wooden, basketball coach of UCLA, was a "bad coach, a very bad coach." Why? Because he does not spend time preparing his athletes for "the world outside." And what is the world outside? "The fans and the press." Hey, wow! *That's* the world outside? It may be for Dick Young and his cohorts, but to a hell of a lot of young athletes the world outside is wars, and rumors of wars, and drugs, and the draft, and racism, and trying to stay even with the cost of food.

But obviously what bugs Dick Young is not Wooden's failure to build character in his charges (instead of, for God's sake, just teaching them how to play winning basketball) but the coach's refusal to lay his kids open to the questioning of sports reporters.

"They build a wall around a young man," says Young about coaches like Wooden.

Well, why not? There are guys who are wordly wise enough to spar with the wiseacres of the press and not let themselves in for idiotic hero-worship or insensitive prying into family affairs or unwarranted "interpretations" of looks, remarks, or careless gripes. But many a kid has been horrified to learn that a newspaper man he had accepted as a friend has taken some "confidential" gripe the kid has muttered and turned it into a headline.

Once I heard Cardinal pitcher Bob Gibson, on TV, reverse roles with a sports interviewer in order to illustrate

what irritated Gibson about such guys. "How much
money do you make?" Bob asked the man. "Do you think
you're worth that much? Are you going to hit the boss for
a raise? Why isn't your wife traveling with you?" And so
on. The interviewer saw the point quickly enough. He sure
as hell did not answer any of the questions.

My own dealings with sportswriters, both in New York
and in San Diego, have been generally free from rancor.
All the same, I have often been irritated by the manner
in which a number of them pretend to inside knowledge
they cannot possibly possess, and by how they build, out
of minor and meaningless events, whole structures of pre-
diction and forecast. A rookie quarterback looks good
in practice and immediately a sportswriter turns out several
hundred words on the probability that the veteran is going
to be traded. Or the veteran has a bad day and the
"experts" of the local press, as if commenting from an
encyclopedic understanding of football, ridicule his stupidity, second-guess his play choices, "interpret" his state of
mind, and even call for his retirement.

Maybe coaches *should* have seminars in dealing with
the press. But if ever I held such a seminar my number
one lesson would consist of one line: "Smile and say as
little as possible." And that would hold until the athlete
had a chance to observe which guys were really out to
write objectively about sports and which were given to
flaunting their own wisdom, their access to inside sources,
and their moral indignation at failures to follow their
advice.

In New York, I had the good luck to know two or
three really good guys, to whom you could talk without fear
that would they turn a pain in the ass into a plan to
organize a mutiny. Paul Zimmerman of the *Post* was
particularly sound—a friendly guy whom you could trust
and who never made out that he knew more about the
subject than you did. Here in San Diego we have a fellow
named Rick Smith, another completely objective, fair-
minded writer who does his job and lets you do yours.
We also have a couple of guys who enjoy posing as
oracles and who can spin out yards of speculation on a

bare minimum of fact. You'd almost think they knew something about football to read what they write.

Before a coach can figure out what has gone wrong on many a play, he has to see the film three or four times, even have the action stopped again and again. Only after such study, by a man who knows exactly what each player is supposed to do, can a coach decide what error of commission or omission led to the interception, the loss, or whatever. But sportswriters, up there in the press box with no knowledge at all of what the play is going to be or what the player-assignments are, do not hesitate to assess blame in a split second and undertake to ream out the transgressor.

Of course on a wide-open play, such as a punt return or a kickoff, mistakes are often easy to spot. But what if a quarterback, trying to get off a pass, is hit by a linebacker just as he lets go of the ball and as a consequence the ball pops free and is intercepted? Was this a lousy play-call? Was it poor performance by the quarterback in failing to hold on to the ball? Was it an instance of lack of maturity—inasmuch as a ground play would have kept the ball in position, say, for a field goal attempt?

The writers have helped to give John Hadl a hard time here. One of the ironies of their treatment is that, at the beginning of the season, when John had a bad few quarters, they marked him as all gone by and suggested he should move out and let me take over. At the end of the season, after John had given several exhibitions of brilliant reading of defenses and crisp performance, and I had grown stale on the bench, the same guys were predicting that *I* would be traded as surplus. (Our rookie quarterback meanwhile had gone into a game and called seven plays without a mistake, marking him, in the writers' eyes, as ready for the first string.)

I think unfair comment often helps stir the fans up to riding a quarterback so he can hardly step on the field without being half drowned in a torrent of boos. John Hadl, I know, at one time had about made up his mind to ask to be traded. And Don Meredith, if he had not been gifted with such a fine sense of proportion, might have been driven into premature retirement by the riding he took in Dallas.

John Hadl once was driven almost to the point of rearranging one writer's kisser after the guy had treated John to two weeks of ignorant comment about John's "inability to win the big ones." Comment of this sort from someone who can assess whether a quarterback's trouble is flat feet, old age, or the failure of the offensive line, is hard enough to handle. But when it comes from a man who cannot tell zone coverage from man-to-man and is offered in a manner that admits no reply, you are bound to begin to contemplate duking it out with the guy right on the grass. John came about as close as I have ever seen him come to letting fly at the man, but he controlled himself finally, contented himself with a simple invitation to the man to go fuck himself, and walked away.

Our situation in San Diego probably is typical of what takes place in many cities. Look at how the sportswriters second-guessed Craig Morton and labeled him over the hill—only to have the guy drag his club into the Superbowl. There must have been something good about what Morton was doing. But the newspaper guys were unable to locate it.

The guys on our club now take special care to tell their unfavorite writer "I don't want to see that in print" whenever they find him listening to what they may say. This writer took a remark by Steve DeLong once, made on the sideline when Steve was still psyched up from a tough loss, and inflated it into a considered judgment by Steve that the whole club was goofing off.

We have learned now that we can tell writers almost anything and have them believe it. "The tight end forgot to hook. They went into a zone against us." It makes no difference. The writer watching the game from his high perch can't even figure out if it happened that way or not.

And we have to resist the constant efforts of some of these guys to pry into affairs that are of no proper concern to them or their readers.

I wonder what would happen if I, in my ignorance,

decided to speculate on why one of the writers spends
so much time with his nose in a highball glass? I have an
idea his mates might resent such public pointing of the
finger. They'd be right, too. But they might all profit from
trying that tight shoe on the *other* foot to see what it feels
like to be psychoanalyzed by self-appointed authorities
whose qualifications are never made public.

A good part of the time, poor performance by the
quarterback can be laid to the failure of the offensive line
to coordinate or carry out its assignments. This was what
happened to John Hadl. His performance grew sharp as
soon as the line-play began to jell. But to the local sports
writers, it was John Hadl all the way—all washed up at
the start of the season and fit only to be traded off, and
one of the best before the season was over.

Lest anyone think I am griping only because we received
poor notices in the press for a losing season, let me tell
what happened during my rookie year. At that time I
listened open-mouthed while a San Diego sportswriter
stood face to face with tight end Jacque MacKinnon and
told Jacque he was "finished as a player" and that if
Jacque thought differently he was only fooling himself.

More recently, one of our local geniuses of the press, who
is great for reporting how "the public" or "the majority of
the fans" may think on whatever subject is under current
discussion, staged a campaign to drive Sid Gilman out of
his coaching job, on the basis of rebellion he had detected
among the season ticket holders. (He must have added up
six phone calls and a dozen postcards to come to his
conclusion, for the truth is that season ticket sales were
running ahead of the year before.) The writer actively
urged the club president, Gene Klein, to "yield" to this
imaginary public demand and send Sid into retirement.
Fortunately, Gene Klein is able to make up his own mind
about the worth of the guys who work for him, so Sid is
going to come back and give us a winner.

But the press campaign against Sid attained such a pitch
that some less assured man might have believed it really
represented the Voice of the People.

It takes a fair amount of arrogance, I think, for a guy

with a superficial knowledge of football to assume the right
to downrap a player and a coach. Activities of this sort
by the writers are bitterly resented by the jocks. I think
the number-one annoyance in every Charger's life is the
presence of the sportswriters. You dare not let one see you
in a treatment room or he is likely to tag you as laid up
for the season. We do have, as I said, one solid citizen
writing sports in San Diego: Rick Smith, who will even
ask you sometimes if you really want a statement printed
as it first sounded. The other guys are quick to grab any
quote and hustle off with it before the player gets a
chance to change his mind.

I know people say that the fans pay the freight and so
they have a right to boo the ballplayers. I won't argue that.
Pro football is show business, and I guess the public has
a right to turn thumbs up or down as they please. As a
matter of fact, I think most ballplayers learn to live with
the boos and some can laugh or even tune them out. In
football the players are not close enough to the customers
to have to put up with the coarse personal riding and the
flinging of small missiles that baseball players are subjected
to in some parks, or the tossing of pennies and nickels on
the ice that the animals at the hockey games go in for.

But the practiced knifing and slicing some sportswriters
take pleasure in can really throw a man completely off
his feed, even affect his play, chiefly because of his frustration at being unable to answer. These guys naturally have
the edge on you, from having exclusive access to the public
forum. And there are guys in the country who are not
above using this edge as a means of managing private
hatchet jobs.

There have been writers, too, who can mess a guy up
completely by building him into a "character" that has no
resemblance to reality at all—putting quotes in his mouth
and inventing antics and opinions for him. A long time ago
I read a story by Al Stump about what the sportswriters
did to a baseball player named Lou Novikoff. Maybe if
Dick Young studied that piece he would understand why
some athletes and some coaches fight shy of opening their
locker-room doors and their hearts to the press. For Lou

was built into an almost idiotic figure, without basis in reality, and practically driven out of his profession.

I do think that today's sportswriters are probably less callous and less arrogant than the ones who made Novikoff's life miserable. I don't believe there are many who would chop a guy up just to keep their readers laughing. But there are some like that still and there are many who lack the humility to question their own grasp of the game they are writing about. Most sportswriters here on the coast have been around long enough to know that a coach does not trade off a quarterback because a rookie looks good in an exhibition. And they have been to enough games and practices to understand that a quarterback does not become a meathead when a lineman misses a block or a receiver fails to go through his pattern. Still, they have taken John Hadl apart for failures that were not his own and they have forecast trades that no one in the management has even dreamed about. Perhaps what is needed, for Dick Young and his colleagues, are seminars where coaches will teach sportswriters how to understand what they see and how to treat young athletes who have not yet attained their emotional growth.

I think athletes can be loused up by unmerited praise as much as they can by criticism. It is easy to tell yourself that some guy who finds fault with your play-calling is a horse's ass. But can you say that about a reporter who compares you to Sammy Baugh and Sid Luckman? I find that I can eat up large helpings of flattery and still have an appetite for more. There must be many other athletes who have been misled by extravagant praise into overlooking their own weaknesses, and goofing off in practice. Praise, of course, is needed by even the best performers. The top coaches never fail to tell a guy when he is doing well. But making a young man into a hero on the basis of a fine exhibition season or a single great performance, or his doings in a secondary league, can set him to thinking he does not need to work any more or that he need not obey the rules laid down for ordinary cats. If anyone had the time to trace the careers of all the springtime heroes in baseball or the pre-season stars

Detach and mail

BALTIMORE WINS THE BLUNDER BOWL

Sports Illustrated

JIM O'BRIEN'S SUPER KICK

CATCH
SPORTS ILLUSTRATED
20 WEEKS FOR ONLY $2.97

Tear out this card and treat yourself to 20 weeks overflowing with sport excitement, color, drama and humor. With this introductory offer for new subscribers only, you'll kick off football '71—both college and pro—and bring the endless dimension and vivid panorama of sport into your home as only SPORTS ILLUSTRATED can.

For 20 weeks, you'll straddle football's 50-yard line and enjoy a sparkling season of golf, tennis, boxing, basketball, skiing, hockey, baseball and horse racing—all the big competitions at their finest. Mail this card today to begin your Introductory Subscription to SPORTS ILLUSTRATED.

Please send me $1 for 20 weeks and bill me later for $2.97
or ☐ Double my savings and send me 40 weeks for $5.94.

Mr.
Mrs.
Miss
_____
(please print)

_____

Address _____ Apt. #

_____

City   State
This offer includes all postage and handling and is good in U.S. only.

S 70211

in football, he would run into several tons of meat and
muscle that have had to spend months or even years
ridding themselves of the conviction that they were two
hops from the Hall of Fame.

Take a look, for example, at what happened to Terry
Bradshaw. How could he possibly have been the man to
lead Pittsburgh to a championship? He had not even
learned to read defenses, let alone acquaint himself with
the peculiarities of his own teammates, when he came
charging in to drive off the bad guys single-handed. In
pre-season games no one is trying too hard to dismember
an offense. Coaches are all experimenting with new ideas,
there are frequent openings in the defense where an accurate passer can lay the ball. But once the bell rings,
it's a bit different.

I think if Terry had not been misled by the snowstorm
of publicity, he would not have had such a disastrous
season, for he would have known right along how much
he had to learn, what he had to work on, and what he
dare not try. But even athletes can be misled, by the ringing
authority with which sports columnists express themselves,
into believing that those guys know as much as the coach.
And someone might also have had time to make note of
the fact that Terry Hanratty, Bradshaw's understudy, had
a hard time throwing a football more than thirty yards.

I think sportswriters on the college beat are generally
pretty considerate of college athletes. At least those I met
in New York always were. They never undertook to pick
flaws in a guy's character or attitude or called for anyone's
demotion from the varsity. But the best of them can sometimes bug a young fellow to distraction, so I cannot blame
a coach who decides he must bar the door to writers.
Even college players are continually checking to see who
is getting the "ink" today. That can become such a major
item in an athlete's life that it may turn into the prime
consideration. Worse than keeping an eye on the sideline to
see how you are going over with the coach is fixing one
eye on the press box to learn if you are receiving your
share of ink.

Dick Young, in the column I mentioned, complained

that Bill Bradley of the New York Knicks could not even accept a "how are you?" from a writer without asking himself what moved the guy to ask that question. Most likely Bill had had first-hand experience with what some writers can whip up on the basis of a careless answer to a question like that. If the player should happen to answer "so-so," he could start a small bonfire on the subject of his physical condition. Or he might find out from next morning's paper that he was sulking over having been benched the night before. And, if I exaggerate, it is merely something I have picked up from long study of Dick Young and his ilk.

It will be argued, of course, that without sportswriters and the fame that sportswriters can build for a player, sports would not be nearly so popular, gate receipts would dwindle, and high salaries disappear. To me that is like arguing that, if it were not for the writers of pornographic literature and the reports in the press of rapes, sex orgies, and illicit romance, public interest in sex would fade away.

Sports came before the writers. Sports stories build circulation and keep the attention of readers. Sports reporters and columnists owe their high salaries to the games, not the other way around. The eager grabbing after inside anecdotes and the exploiting of the private lives of sports heroes is not motivated by a desire to improve the financial standing of the heroes but to attract the attention of the fans who are hungry for a chance to feel close to a famous figure, or even to see him brought down nearer to their own level.

I think it is healthy that the TV industry has moved in the direction of putting more ex-athletes in charge of commenting on and interpreting the play. I notice that the athlete-announcers are a lot slower to pretend to infallibility, and will even point out their own mistakes and laugh at them. They help the viewers understand what they have just seen and while they do have a disconcerting way of describing a football player as "shaken up" when he may have been decapitated, they make an obvious effort to find out what *really* happened and describe it. Of course, they don't have to fill up a column every day and so may not be as pressed as the writers are to make as much smoke as they can with whatever tiny bits of fire they can pick up.

No professional athlete should bitch about fans. They do pay the freight and they would be there to make the game profitable even if there were no sportswriters to permit them to read all about the game they just got through watching.

There have been moments, however, when I have permitted fans to bug me slightly, although I have taken care not to show it. Once when I was eating dinner I had a well-dressed man of 35 or so aproach and ask me for an autograph. The giving out of autographs has always seemed to me the least of what I owe to fans, so even when people stop me, as this man did, with my fork halfway to my mouth, I do not let myself become annoyed. I don't seek new ways of sneaking out of the stadium so as to duck the crowds of kids with paper to sign—as some veteran players do. And I make my regular appearances on the local banquet circuit as part of my duty, without complaint.

But this guy! He took a little autograph book out of his pocket, proffered his pen, and told me: "My son wants your autograph if you don't mind, Marty. He's one of your biggest fans. I really don't know why. Because frankly I don't think you're all that good!"

Jesus! What kind of upbringing did that bird have? Is he one of the jerks who has been told by his psychiatrist always to express his feelings truthfully, lest he start to develop a tic or something? I still don't know what kept me from tossing my salad in his face. But I muttered something or other and signed the book. And then the guy gave me his card and said: "I'd appreciate it, Marty, if you could get *John Hadl's* picture for me and have him autograph it."

So I put his card in my pocket and nodded and said I would. But I never did.

I have been slightly pissed too when the hangers-on who are always around after a game or in the regular eating place, and who will hardly let you draw a breath with their "How are you, Marty? How's it going? Here, I'd like you to meet a friend of mine"—when they, after a losing game, will suddenly fade away. All right, so they prefer winners. But I prefer fans who are with you in foul weather as well as fair.

Of course, even the best of fans grow a little hostile sometimes when you keep on losing. They quite often exhibit justified annoyance themselves when the players do not seem to take the losses to heart. Bob Babich and I have been at dinners where the attitude was as chilly as if the air-conditioning were geared too high. Once after we had been swamped by the Rams—our fourth loss in a row—the two of us made an appearance at a Kiwanis club dinner. We had tried hard to cook up little jokes to tell and gags to pull on each other, and amusing "inside" anecdotes to relate. But my God what a frost! I would labor to tell a carefully prepared joke and not a single snort of laughter did I raise. Our "funny anecdotes" were received in unbroken gloom. The gags we pulled on each other brought back only icy stares. It soon developed, from the questions we were asked, that the men in the room did not see anything funny about our losing streak and were definitely turned off by our appearing to take it so lightly.

I couldn't be *mad* at them about that. Bob and I felt just like a couple of asses and we learned right then to take our fans' disappointment more seriously.

There is one form of pest we on the Chargers have not yet had any trouble with. We have never had cigar-faced characters sidle up to us and try to get inside information on the condition of our players or the possible line-ups. God knows we have been warned often enough of the possibility that slick professional great-guys may seek our acquaintance and try to use us as sources of information for the setting of gambling odds. But it just hasn't happened yet.

The security guys from the Commissioner's office visit us annually and offer us a list of five or six local taverns and hang-outs where gamblers and other doubtful characters—including, of all things, prostitutes!—may be found. These places, they urge us solemnly, should be avoided at all costs. But telling our gang where whores are likely to be found is like "warning" a bunch of teen-age kids which books and movies are most likely to corrupt their morals. Some of the guys holler out requests for the full addresses of these off-limits joints. And nobody really believes the assurances that the official gumshoes are on our trails— ever. I don't think Pro Football is ready to lay out money on squads of full-time detectives. At least not when it cannot even "afford" full-time officials.

It does seem ludicrous that the National League, with the tremendous profits it must be making, the enormous sums it lays out in public relations, and the fat salaries it pays in the central offices, still cannot pay officials enough so that they do not have to hold week-day jobs too. Yet there is not an official at any of the league games who is not a part-time operator. They all have other work that involves them through the week. And a few of the players are convinced that some of the officials must have their minds on their regular jobs while the games are going on.

I think one of the first things that strikes a rookie in the big league is the almost total lack of respect shown to many of the officials by the players on the sideline and by the coaches. In every game there is a steady flow of sometimes obscene comment from the sidelines to the officials. The best officials simply close their ears to it, concerning themselves entirely with what takes place on the field of play. Besides, when an official gets too close to the sideline, the shouts of "You missed that one, you bastard!" suddenly die down.

Most of the officials realize that football is such an emtional game that the players and coaches have to have some outlet to reduce their head of steam. When someone on the field offers comments too rough or too personal, the Man is likely to throw a flag. But flak from the side-lines—that's part of the job.

Still, you do see more and more calls that are so out-rageous it is impossible to be still about them. Even TV commentators, who are superstitious about second-guessing the officials, have to struggle sometimes to keep from commenting on the obvious—a receiver called out of bounds when he is in-bounds by half the length of his body; or some potential receiver grabbed and held on to with both hands. Of course if officials wanted to be technical they could practically bring a game to a halt by calling illegal use of the hands on every play, for the sparring in the pit sometimes degenerates into clutching and grabbing, and pass protection is often improved by a partially extended arm. But, just as basketball officials have learned to allow limited and unimportant contact regardless of the rules, so pro football officials have learned to overlook some of the less important violations that do not seriously impede a play.

But still you see some petty violations called that will bring a drive to a halt, or call back a score. Tripping, for instance. Practically any lineman who uses the length of his body to block out an opponent is likely to have another opponent stumble over his extended leg. I don't think that sort of "tripping" is what rule-makers were worried about when they made the rule. But I have seen important plays turned around when an accident like that brings a flag.

At other times, officials have either overlooked or just failed to call violations that stop a play dead. In our game with Baltimore I watched an official blow a call that practically cost us the game. It was not that he didn't *see* the violation. Almost everyone in the park, including the official, saw the Baltimore offensive tackle, protecting the passer, take hold of our defensive end with both hands and hold him out. The official grabbed for his flag. He missed it. He reached for it again. He missed it again. The third time he got hold of it and started to pull it out. By then the pass was away and completed, the ball dead, the play over. He let his flag stay in his pocket. Just what motivated him I don't know. Maybe he was afraid he'd look foolish or get yelled at. But he got yelled at anyway.

Still, his failure to call the holding was not quite so raw as a call we were the victims of later in the season. This was in the Oakland game when our Bobby Howard took a pass away from Fred Biletnikoff, and took it clean away, as the films showed. The closest official miscalled it himself. He agreed that Bobby had got the ball but he called the play out of bounds and so incomplete—leaving Oakland in possession. But then an official *30 yards away* overruled the first call. It was in-bounds, he said. And it had been a "simultaneous catch." On such a catch, the ball goes to the offensive man. It was a gain of more than forty yards for Oakland, and it meant a touchdown two or three plays later.

This call was so bad the papers were full of it next day. Stop-action photographs showed Bobby taking the ball in both hands while Biletnikoff, in full stride, was vainly reaching for the ball with his left hand and missing it. They showed Biletnikoff, still in full stride, bowling into Bobby, knocking him down, rolling over him, and coming to a stop out of bounds. And they showed Bobby, safely in-bounds, bouncing up from the turf with the ball held aloft. Granted that one official did have his view partially obscured by Biletnikoff's body, I still don't see how such a call would ever have been made.

Of course, these were not the only calls we had to gripe about. There were at least a dozen more. But these were two that would never have happened if the officials had been properly trained and if they had had some standards to go by. An official should be trained to have the courage of his convictions and *never* to change his call just because he can't get the flag out. And there should be some definite protocol about always letting the man closest to the play call it as he sees it or getting another official's view only when he needs it.

What's the harm in hiring officials on a full-time basis? They could devote their empty time during the week to studying films of the teams they are going to work with on Sunday. They could also work out at scrimmages to learn their own trade better, to practice being in position for whatever plays might develop. And to practice getting the flags out of their pockets.

I have never had any real run-ins with officials and generally have fared well. One or two of the veteran officials have been helpful to me in learning my job. In the beginning, for instance, I had a habit of pulling out of contact with the center just before the snap, from eager-

ness to get a quick start. Then one official came close to
me after one play and warned me: "Keep your hands in
there, son, or I am going to call a violation on you."

You can believe I took special care after that not to
lose contact with the center's pants until the ball had been
snapped. This warning made me a better quarterback and
I have never lost my respect for that particular official.
When he throws a flag, I believe him, even when my own
eyes tell me he could have been wrong.

But all these—meat-headed sportswriters, angry fans,
inept officials—are of very small account compared to the
one topic that is almost never spoken of seriously among
pro athletes. That is *Money*. In this line of work a man
becomes very conscious of the supersonic speed at which
"Time's Winged Chariot" can pull up behind you and
start honking to get by. Quarterbacks generally don't have
to fret as much about that, because they are always the
best paid members of the squad and have long careers.
But the other guys have a much shorter season for making
hay.

It is traditional that when the team goes out together
the quarterback picks up the check. He has the big bank-
roll. And the guys who slave in the pit are the ones who
keep the enemy off his back. How can a man refuse to
stand the drinks for the guys who are up there pouring
out blood and sweat to keep the quarterback right side up?

But the other players whose take does not match the
quarterback's, on our club at least, feel almost without
exception that they are underpaid and overworked. The
odd part of this is that, if you go by the figures the
Players' Association put out, our club is one of the best
paid in the game. It may simply be that it is so *hard* to
negotiate a contract with our management that the players
actually shrink from the job, and so often go along griping
to themselves that they have been had.

It is not often that players talk about salaries among
themselves, except in a joking manner. But money is
always on everyone's mind and everyone is concerned with
whether any particular teammate is signed or unsigned.
When a man plays out his option with us it is always a

matter of money. And when guys *do* talk about negotiating for more money, they describe the task of getting any sort of raise as "Mission Impossible." So they probably stay sore all season, when they might have been mollified with a small raise or at least a friendly interview.

As an illustration of the difficulties of getting extra bread for a season's work, the guys, laughing bitterly, will tell the experience of our outsized defensive lineman, Ron Billingsley, when he tried for an extra $1000. Coach Gilman allowed that for him to ask for a raise was ridiculous after Ron had had "three dogshit seasons in a row!"

"Why you ought to play three years for nothing to make it up to us!" the coach declared. Then, after a session of snapping and snarling, Ron came out with what must be the smallest raise ever offered a man in this line of work—$500.

I am not going to say that Ron's play was affected because I think he plays his heart out anyway, out of pride and loyalty to his team. But I do think there is some sapping of morale when relations between player and management can become this rancorous. A player should be allowed his dignity, even if it costs the club a few hundred more. And I believe anyway that a guy's salary should be increased with each new contract, as long as he hangs on to his job. It is not always the extra few bucks that matter. It is the feeling that the management wants to play fair. Someone said once that injustice (or even imagined injustice) rather than poverty is what makes men rebel. There sure as hell is no poverty on the Chargers. But some players do feel there has been injustice.

6

Killers All!

The proper posture for a guy in my position, I suppose, is quiet gratitude that, after five months on the waiting list, I was enrolled in the National Guard and now can take my army in small doses with no need to wallow ass-deep in shit through Viet Nam rice paddies while somebody tries to blow holes in me. Well, I am happy I didn't have to travel 7000 miles to help swell some outfit's body count. But I am not going to recommend the National Guard as a rest cure, a reform school, or a recreational facility. They play with live guns in the Guard and, even though there is the standard amount of chickenshit, there is sweat and discipline and getting your hands dirty.

The regular army, I hear tell, has a larger quota of gung-ho types who divide the world into good guys and bad guys and name all Orientals slopes and gooks. In the Guard we may have officers who are closer to the real world. We get a share of the simplistic ones. But they are offset by the men who have to help get the world up in the morning and put it safely to bed at night.

There is of course, in the Guard as in the army, a lot of make-work and lost motion. Someone asked me once to keep track of everything I did in the National Guard in the spring of 1970 and write it down in a diary, "even the petty stuff." Do you know there were days when I was unable to think of *anything* I had done that wasn't petty? But then there are complex drills and real excitements. There are good guys to meet from all over the state and rituals that can raise a laugh. It may be that chickenshit is

90

always a peace-time army's most important product. But in the Guard, where at least you can count the days until you get out, there are compensations.

My biggest day in the Guard was the day I set a new record for throwing the 16-ounce grenade (about as heavy as three baseballs). We were built up to this exercise by solemn warnings that the grenade is a "weapon of destruction," that there is but a four- to seven-second delay between pulling the fuse and detonation (provided the handle is released) and that there have been many scary accidents. One poor slob, the drill sergeant told us, opened his hand slightly after pulling the plug. This of course, released the handle and started the timing mechanism. He held on to the grenade and of course was soon turned into fragments. Within seven seconds. It was hard to know whether to believe this story or not.

There were 130 of us huddled on the safe side of a protective wall as one man after another advanced to throw—and to duck. Flying bits of metal from exploded grenades flew over our heads and the bullshit flowed even more freely.

You have to "hang on tight" to the little missile and "for God's sake don't drop it" or the whole outfit will be totaled. You have to be damn sure to "get good distance" on your throw or even the wall might not save you!

Most of this crap peters out as a man moves nervously forward to try his throw. You hug the little pineapple to your chest, you pull the pin, you r'ar back with your throwing arm behind you, à la John Wayne, and you let fly—and duck! There is a hell of a bang and the man next at bat feels a flutter in his stomach. But once everyone has had his turn they all look at each other and wonder what the hell the fuss was all about. It was not much different from tossing a cherry-bomb into the street and listening to the pop.

My own experience at the grenade range was somewhat more fulfilling. I had not known there was such a thing as a "record" for throwing the grenade and I was doubtful as hell about trying for it. Risk my unwarmed-up throwing arm for some horseshit record? I couldn't be that crazy.

But I got ribbing enough from my mates to tempt me to try it anyway and I took a somewhat cautious heave toward the 95-meter mark—the record. The grenade fell ten meters short.

Just ten meters short when I was not even trying? Now the competitive urges began to churn in my gut. Despite the voice that kept warning me I was a horse's ass to try it, I asked for another grenade.

I pulled the pin. I held the little object to my chest, where my heart seemed to pound against it. I hauled off. I threw! The instructor yanked me down behind the wall! and BOOM! A new record! 101 meters for tossing the 16-ounce grenade! A handshake from the C. O.! A free coke! My name would go down in National Guard history, while young men yet unborn would stare out at the mark I had made and marvel!

The biggest deal for most of the guys, however, was the night infiltration course. There would be live fire over our heads, streaking tracers that were really a thrill to watch, like markings of a fiery pencil, all drawn with beautiful flowing precision on the black sky. This was the first time we had trained with other companies. There were five different units in all and the presence of these rivals seemed to charge up every heart—to the point where we chanted greetings back and forth in the form of irreverent marching songs, like these:

> "I *don't* go out with *girls* any more.
> I *live* a life of *dan*ger!
> I *stay* at home and *play* with myself.
> *Whee!* I'm a *Ran*ger!"

and

> "A *yell*ow bird with a *yell*ow bill,
> *Perched* upon my *win*dowsill.
> I *lured* it in with a *piece* of bread
> And *slammed* the *window on* its *fucking* head!"

and one with a dozen verses:

> Hi, Ho, Diddley Bop!
> I *wish* I was *back* on the block!
> *With* a razor *in* my hand.
> I *wanta* be a *fighti*ng man!
> Your *left*, your *left*, your *left*, right *left*!
> Hi, Ho, Diddley Bop!
> I wish I was back on the block!
> With a joint in my hand!
> I wanta be a smoking man!

Each company "presented arms" to the other, meanwhile, by freely offering them "the finger."

Then it grew dark and several demonstrators made their way through a small facsimile of the course while the instructors explained what they were doing and how *we* were to do it—and we paid scant attention.

Once the demonstration is over and it is nearly dark the instructor shouts out to the whole assemblage:

> "*Are you ready?*"

The answer, from the several hundred thoats, is a howling war-cry that could chill the blood of a Sioux.

Immediately the night expoldes—red tracers whistle across the sky. Bombs shatter. A flare bursts silently high overhead—and damned if we are not all as charged up as kids at an old-fashioned Fourth of July. The instructor asks again:

> "*Still ready?*"

The whole mob rises to its feet, M-16's held high, and roars like a thousand maddened buffalo. We all move, hearts pounding, to the retaining wall. A half dozen guys suddenly discover their bladders are overloaded and one man in his excitement studiously pisses on a drill sergeant's foot. The sergeant's angry bellow is drowned by our delighted laughter.

The whistle blows! Over the wall and away! It is amazing how different those guns sound when you are in front of the muzzles. The racket seems to burst the ears. Men are bent low and scuttling like scared monkeys through the half-light. Here and there clusters of trainees huddle together, their faces dead white in the light of the flare.

The first obstacle is barbed wire, where men must lie on their backs, holding up the wire with one hand and M-16 in the other, while pushing themselves along with their heels. You have to be careful not to raise your knees too high or—Jesus! For the first time in my life I curse the fate that made me six-feet-four. The goddamn barb has gashed my knee. Next there is a log. No sweat. And a trench. An easy jump. More barbed wire. I have to slow down again, lie once more on my back. Now suppose some jerk crawling behind me should push his bayonet into my thigh! But I get through unscathed.

Then it's over and nobody is badly hurt. Maybe a few twisted ankles, where guys missed their footing when jumping the trench, or minor barbed wire nicks, or muscle pulls from leaping with too much oomph.

That was about all the really rugged work we experienced. But in many ways the whole four months have been depressing. Here there are guys who *hate* the army, as much as any jailbird ever hated the bars that held him back. Yet they were losers who would probably have to give their whole lives to this. No escape into the dream world of pro football for them.

There are not many blacks in the National Guard. In the first place, there not many blacks who know how to apply or have advisers to help them. And even among the black pro athletes who might have made it, there are a number who take a more fatalistic attitude than the whites. Get the goddam thing over with, they say. Take the active service all at once, whack, and trust to luck to come out of it alive. I think this "let's get it over with" practice is far more common in the ghettos than among the middle-class, where you have learned that if you put off an evil day long enough it may never arrive at all. A black man who is also poor knows that *nothing* is going to keep hard luck away forever.

What sickened me most about the whole deal, I think, was the attitude of many of the Permanent Party, the lifers who seem to have as much enthusiasm for war as I have for football. Is football supposed to be our Roman circus? I think we may find out that it is *battle* that we

enjoy most. These guys back from Viet Nam told their
tales with relish that could not be faked. There were men
who had shot fleeing villagers in the back—old men and
women ("Well, for Christ's sake, they *had* to be VC!")
—and recounted all the details as if they were telling about
a deer hunt. They shot prisoners to boost the confirmed
dead count. You "couldn't take them along." And anyway,
"Charlie would have done the same if he'd caught me."
There were men who had brought in necklaces made of
dried ears, cut from Cong bodies.

No doubt there was a percentage of bullshit in all the
stories, but what grabbed me was the delight these guys
took in living the experiences over again. It was just as
if they were ticking off their sexual triumphs—and many
of the kid trainees ate up the war stories with as much
appetite as if they had been anecdotes about screwing.

Maybe some fans do go to football games to glory in
seeing a player receive a "good hit" that might put him out
of the game for life. But what of these guys, who teach
their admirers that murder is great fun if it is done whole-
sale? Does anyone mount investigations to learn if they are
charged up with greenies or stoned on skag? Do we have
a Commissioner to pry into the behavior of our professional soldiers, to insure that they are living up to the
glorious traditions of the Game of War?

The Guard officers were of varying types. Most of them
would pass in a hip crowd for hopeless squares, for they
were devoted to the old-fashioned virtues and kept their
hair cut short. They were not, or not all, as mindless and
as gung-ho as the regular army types, and I imagine this
may be because the Guard has something more in its
future than merely turning live people into dead bodies.
The Guard also does rescue and relief work, polices disaster areas, brings food to the hungry, and sets up camps
where people made homeless by fire, flood, or earthquake
can find shelter, so you get the feeling that there is more
to serving your country than just pointing your gun at the
chosen enemy and blasting him into the next world.

There was one guy at Fort Ord who must have been
trying to fashion himself after a movie character. He had

a shaved head and was shined up like the front end of a new Cadillac. He *loved* war. He had actually, for Christ's sake, "volunteered" his unit for service in Viet Nam and could think of no more holy mission in life than killing all Communists.

What did depress me was the number of kids in the outfit who embraced the idea that we were there to become "professional killers"—a sort of legalized Murder, Inc. There was some talk, toward the end of our stay, that there might be demonstrations near the fort, so we were confined to the area. Even so, there were some among us who yearned openly for a chance to "shoot some of the goddamned hippy bastards." Shooting somebody begins to sound so trifling and routine after listening to the Permanent Party heroes. During our infiltration course, as we looked back at the black silhouettes firing the tracer bullets, it seemed a simple task indeed to get one in our sights and "do him a job!" They were not humans at all, merely targets.

On our march back, after our work under the curtain of tracer bullets, the company was full of heroes who were convinced now that they had been "under fire" and had found it easy to take. All of a sudden shooting and being shot at seemed routine—not at all like killing your fellow man but just the carrying out of a simple assignment. God help these heroes if they ever find themselves in a spot where those tracer bullets are really trying to feel out the way to their flesh!

Of course the deadly boredom of army life eventually got to the heroes too. Moping around, doing petty clean-up jobs and looking after the comfort of the officers was no way to keep grown men from going bananas. It was too painfully obvious that much of our "training" was a sheer waste. We had detailed instruction and work on hand-to-hand combat, for instance. Then our instructor solemnly warned us never to try out any of our lessons except "as a last resort" and never to count on overcoming an enemy with any of these magic blows and holds, unless he was unconscious or, for Christ's sake, already dead!

So, well before those long and deadly four months were over, everybody, gung-ho guys and normal human beings alike, were joining in the standard chorus:

> "Two more weeks of polishing brass,
> Then Fort Ord can kiss my ass!"

I had been in touch with Charley Waller by telephone several times, to make sure my job was still there and to get a line on what the practice schedule was. The word I received was cheering indeed. There seemed a better than even chance that I might be dividing the quarterback job with John Hadl, so my spirits remained reasonably high as my army training drew to a close without my having wrecked my passing hand on any barbed wire or been lamed by an accidental jab from a bayonet. (These possibilities had actually been much on my mind.) The only danger now seemed to be that the Guard might be called out by one of our glorious leaders to take potshots at protesters somewhere. If *that* happened, God help me! It might mean the end of pro football for me. It would certainly cost me a whole season, the season in which I hoped to move up to first string.

And from the looks of some of our chosen leaders throughout the state and nation, there seemed always a strong chance that one of them would decide to make himself a hero by dealing out live bullets the way they had at Kent State.

For some reason, my private picture of the true state of politics in our country was a view I had had of the Governor of the Sovereign State of Georgia grinning like a toy monkey as he pedaled his bicycle *backwards* around a football field between the halves!

7

Here Comes the Devil!
Watch the Grass Die!

After we beat the Chicago Bears in Chicago in 1970, Sid Gilman came to visit us in the "quarterback's room" (before the game John Hadl had remarked to me that the little cubicle we had been given to suit up in was, appropriately, "a remodeled shithouse"). Sid patted John heartily on the back.

"When you play that way," Sid declared, "I love you!" Then he started back into the main locker room. Just as he was at the door, he turned and chuckled. "But when you lose," he added, "I hate you!"

I wonder if Sid realizes that players often feel that way about coaches, too. I am sure he must. It is a cinch that a driving coach like Lombardi, for instance, who used to think nothing of humiliating a quarterback at the top of his lungs on the practice field, earned the "love" of his players by making them into winners. If he had taken their hides off as he did, had ignored their injuries, and played such obvious favorites in applying disciplinary fines— and had still *lost,* he'd have had the most rebellious locker-room in the league. But when a man is yelling and cursing and sweating to turn you into a champion, with a whole extra year's salary as the prize, it is easy to forgive him for whatever minor cruelties he may subject you to.

Anyone who has ever tried to condition himself without the help of a trainer or a slave-driver knows it cannot be done—except by those rare fanatics who look on their

98

bodies as their enemies. Every normal athlete, no matter how dedicated, needs someone to push him to the limits of his endurance—in order that he may extend those limits. (Even Carl Yastrzemski, to get back into playing shape, had to hire a "personal conditioner" to supervise his workouts and, I suppose, to rap his knuckles when he reached for those second helpings.) A coach who courts the "love" of his players by easing up on them, tolerating the goofoffs on the practice field, and joining them in their dissipations may very well be a great guy. But he will be a lousy football coach.

Sid Gilman is a good coach. He will never own the love of all his players, and I am sure he will not lie awake nights fretting over that. Players respect Sid for his knowledge and, when things are going well, they let his sarcasms run off their backs—he is so obviously pouring out his own heart in the effort to come in first.

It is funny. When the club is winning, players who have been snarling back at the coach (under their breaths) will begin to comment out loud that the Old Man has changed, has "mellowed." They never seem to consider that maybe *they* have changed. One day they may be growling "Here comes the Devil! Watch the grass die!" when the coach heaves into sight. And a few weeks later they may be ready to clobber some guy who has tried to do the coach dirt.

There are some coaches who win the devotion of all their players (or almost all) and hang on to it even when the club is losing; they do this despite the fact that they drive their players to the very edge of their physical capacity. But I don't think these are the coaches who *try* to be popular. They are usually men, like George Allen, who start out with an attractive personality and add to that a dedication to the job that is bound to win the respect of every man on the squad.

Such guys can be the toughest disciplinarians in the world (there are not many more strict than Allen), sweat their players until they drop, and impose strict curfews and limits on their dissipations. But as long as they are *fair,* that is, just, in the application of their rules, take care never to humiliate a guy in public, act friendly as well as firm, and do not ask any man to work harder than the coach himself does, they will have most of the players with them, win or lose. This devotion will be the rallying point of a team that has been taking beating after beating, and it may help unite the squad so they can pull themselves together and start winning again.

Still, there are some coaches who just are not made to be popular. They are so burned up with desire to win that they seem half angry most of the time, practically never hand out any praise, and can't restrain their caustic comments when something goes wrong. For a man who is made that way to try to turn himself into a charmer is ludicrous; most of them, by the time they reach the pros, have more sense than to try. But there are coaches who have made a success in subordinate jobs through their ability to meet the players on their own level and their complete lack of affectation and vanity. Then they may get promoted to head coach and suddenly seem to lose their touch completely.

Something like that happened, I think, to Charley Waller, who is one of the best guys alive—good-natured, smart, and well-liked by all the players. But when he became head coach he was not satisfied just to be plain Charley Waller. He must have felt he needed to change himself into a more positive type, or something. As a result he began to contradict himself and became consistently inconsistent. For instance, in one breath he might promise the squad that he would not point a finger at any particular player. Then a a few minutes later he would be carried away with his irritation at some dereliction and would begin to lay into the "losers" (everyone knew which ones he meant) who, he promised, would not be around much longer if they did not change their ways.

An experienced head coach knows when he has to correct a player but he soon learns that scolding him in public just causes irritation and rebellion. When an experienced player does something wrong, he knows it just as well as the coach does. He does not need to be yelled at to fix the error in his consciousness. He just needs to be told what he *should* have done, or how he could have avoided the error.

And he should be told that without recriminations, preferably in private. When I pitched that ball out in the wrong direction in the New York game, I did not have to have Charley bitch to me about it. I had already kicked my own ass hard.

But coaches have to learn, the same as quarterbacks. Charley was trying hard, buying books on the subject, going to classes. The one thing his books did not tell him was that he should *be himself*. As Sid Gilman remains wholly himself—despite occasional promises not to blow his top at anyone—and thus remains effective, Charley should have kept on being the same good-natured, sympathetic, fair-minded guy we all admired. He is not made to be a Vince Lombardi type. Some guys drive. Other guys lead. Some lead by force of example and exhortation. Others lead by patience and persuasion.

So there really is not any one "profile" of a successful coach. Hank Stram is acknowledged by the players who worked for him—even the ones who did not care for him —to be one of the ablest coaches in the business. Some guys will make fun of the plaintive way he has with his players—his "Geez, guys, don't you want to win? Don't you like me?" But they all agree he can teach them about football and they respond to his fair-mindedness and consistency in applying discipline. (He is one of the few coaches who will not tolerate chin whiskers or sideburns.) And they approve of his method of doing his fault-finding in private.

George Allen is a real cheer-leader. Instead of huddling with his assistants during a game to work out diagrams of plays that might work, he stands on the sideline, yelling encouragement, shaking hands, pounding backs, doing all he can to keep the players' emotions at a high pitch. He almost never sends a play in to his quarterback.

Tom Landry, on the other hand, is almost completely without visible emotion during a game. Sometimes he may call out encouragement in a well-modulated voice and sometimes he may pat his hands lightly together. But most of the time he is the perfect wooden Indian, who just watches, plans, corrects, and perfects. He is probably the most inventive of all the coaches—except that Stram shows more defensive originality. And he, like Stram, has brought his team into the Superbowl by being himself.

Lombardi of course did everything "wrong" as far as handling men is concerned. He bawled them out, even ridiculed them in public, tried to make them believe their injuries were imaginary, and otherwise violated the rules on How to be a Successful Coach. But he was the most successful in the business. It was not his methods alone that brought success. It was his burning sincerity. He did not yell at his players to blame them for his own failings or to work off his frustrations. He just poured out his fierce and ingrained desire to win and the players, even while they hated him for it, responded to him too.

Alex Webster does not pretend to be any great strategist or even a born leader. He is just a solid, fair-minded guy who puts on no airs and is completely on the level with the guys who work for him. While he will never out-think Tom Landry, or out-shout Vince Lombardi, or set an example of leadership, he unites the team through their devotion to him.

I don't suppose any of Paul Brown's players feels that Paul is one of the boys. I doubt if there are many who are stirred to extra effort through their personal devotion to a kindly old father-figure. But Paul Brown's big asset, besides his brilliance as a strategist and his abilities as a teacher, is his unfailing fairness. Guys may come from his club feeling that he worked them too hard or criticized them too severely. But none of them ever feels that Brown was anything but just in his dealings with them, for he plays no favorites and exhibits no prejudices. He will not even say a bad word about men who have vilified him.

There is one coach I know little about, except that some men who have dealt with him think he is the noblest of them all. That is Lou Saban of Denver, and he has earned his reputation as a fine guy to work for by being open-handed with his players. This business of money, as I said earlier, naturally has a strong influence on a player's morale. Sometimes a coach or general manager can give a player the feeling of having been fairly treated—without actually throwing away too much of the club's money. When Don Horn was traded to the Broncos, he came to Denver with his mind made up he was not going to negotiate—that he would just scout out the territory and postpone his contract negotiation until some more propitious moment, after he had consulted all his advisers. But Lou Saban disarmed him completely.

"We'll pay you double whatever you've been getting," Lou said. "We'll find you a house and we'll move your whole family here at our expense." Don, who had been used to some fairly flint-eyed bargaining with his bosses, was overwhelmed and signed the deal without delay. It was only much later that he began to ask himself if he could not have got more if he had negotiated a bit. But he certainly never felt he had been unfairly dealt with. The impression he carried home was that the Broncos dearly wanted him on their side and were ready to go to some lengths to make sure he was content.

There is also a story about a negotiating session Saban had with Dave Costa, an amicable discussion that resulted in a modest advance in salary. But when Costa started out the door, Lou Saban called to him. "Come here," he said. "I've got something for you!" Costa walked back and took the paper Lou was holding out. It was a check for $5000. "You had a great year," said Lou. "We rated you highest of the linemen."

Treatment of that sort is great for building a guy's team spirit, believe me.

Naturally, you get most of your ideas about other coaches from the guys who have worked for them, and usually those are the guys who have been traded off and so they can be counted on to carry some sort of grudge against the man who traded them. Whatever *kind* words you hear about any enemy coach therefore are usually sincere.

You hear hardly any kind words about one guy—Norm Van Brocklin, who is fiery, moody, and unpredictable. He can singe the hair off a guy's back as well as Lombardi ever could, while lacking Lombardi's total dedication. The Dutchman apparently dearly wants to win. But his personality is so volatile that it is hard for him to stay right on the single track to success. The players who have suffered under him used to tell you: "If he comes on the field with a cup of coffee in his hand, stay clear of him!" Apparently he was then ready to disembowel even the best man on the squad if the player happened to set his feet wrong when he lined up. But if he trotted out on the field without his coffee, grabbed up a football, and immediately bounced it off the back of some player's head, then the practice was going to be fun. Still, growling or laughing, the Dutchman is a holler-holler guy who apparently likes to do his "correcting" at the top of his voice.

I have never heard a guy say he wanted to play for Van Brocklin, but there are a number who would like to play for Stram—mainly because they like his theory of defense and respect his knowledge of the game. Almost everyone thinks well of Allen and Lou Saban and no one would be upset about being traded to either of them. Paul Brown is looked on in much the same way. The players know he runs a rough regime but still they feel he is the smartest in the game and operates on the theory that football is fun.

The black players generally were uneasy abut playing in the Southern cities, but more for the anticipated difficulty of finding decent quarters and leading an unimpeded life than for any prejudice they expected to run into on the team. There was only one coach, Wally Lemm, who had a reputation of making things tough for the black players. He seemed offended when black players were seen in public with white girls and he would, the blacks said, try to make their lives miserable thereafter. Undoubtedly there are other guys who nurse some prejudice in their hearts. Many coaches are basically squares, as are most of the older guys from the big football factories, and it would be against nature if they did not retain some of the anti-black feeling that used to be rampant among the country-club set. But those who still cling to any of it seem mostly to express it in private, if at all.

Surely the best coaches work hard to be absolutely even-handed in their dealings with all the guys, whatever their skin shade. As a matter of fact, I believe a really knowledgeable coach realizes that he often has to deal more carefully with black players than with white. Black players are sensitive, from lifelong experience, to any slights visited on the brothers and you can't conceal from them even the unconscious outcroppings of racist feelings. If a black guy is going to be downgraded, a coach with any sensitivity will take care that the rest of the club understands exactly why, so there is not even a faint hint of favoritism or prejudice. Black men long ago learned to squint a skeptical eye at white men who assured them that they "did no special favors for anyone—black or white!" This was too often a way of saying that, as usual, they would continue to hand the black man the shitty end of the stick.

One coach who is well-liked but who is considered overwhelmed by his own quarterback is Weeb Ewbank. Everyone seems to agree that the man who runs the offense there is not Ewbank but Namath. The Jets, however, have a hell of a good defense too, and Namath surely doesn't run that. And if Ewbank has decided that Joe can fire up the team better and pick the defenses apart more skillfully, then he is being a good coach to let Joe take over those departments. White shoes, llama rug, and all, Joe is a down-to-earth guy, thoroughly dedicated to football, who has more than once demonstrated his ability to figure out ways to beat the best. It would be insanity for the Jets not to make full use of his skills, on the sideline or on the field.

For myself, I'd just as soon play for Ewbank, although I would prefer being first-string for Sid Gilman. I like the way Weeb has his offensive linemen block on the line instead of dropping off two or three steps before setting up to protect the passer. This gives the quarterback instant depth and allows him to set up sooner.

I have heard a number of players on different teams express a desire to play for George Allen—mainly because Allen sets great value on experience and holds on to his veterans, while other coaches are quick to run in rookies when a veteran seems to be slowing up or getting hurt more often. With Allen a player has more security. Experience is a priceless asset in Allen's figuring, so the longer a guy has been around the better he is, provided he can still perform. I can understand how playing for a man with that philosophy can take some of the flutter out of a guy's stomach when he sees the rookies outrun him.

As a quarterback, I have a sort of built-in security. I don't allow that anyone can do things that I can't, through application, learn to do, and I expect to be active in the game for no less than fifteen seasons, perhaps even twenty. But running backs, who can never go through three seasons in a row without some injury, go very quickly in this business and must always wonder if any one year could be their last. Linemen and defensive backs last longer but they too always feel vulnerable when the new crop of draft-choices moves in.

If a rookie shoves a veteran out of his job, when the older man still has some good seasons left, it has a depressing effect on the whole club, for naturally all the long-time players begin to fret about their own futures. So Allen's method of clinging to the veterans has a good effect on team morale too. It may be that competition for jobs on a club makes every man fight harder. But Allen has a way of getting full effort out of his charges even though he does not threaten them every week with loss of their jobs. He is known as a straightforward guy who never fails to show his appreciation of honest effort. I imagine he is the man that veteran linebackers would most like to be a traded to.

It is inevitable that a coach's personality should be reflected by his team. Joe Kapp's knock-them-down philosophy, and his obvious joy in physical contact, was an accurate expression of Bud Grant's own approach to the game. While Bud, like practically every pro coach, teaches a good sound strategy, his chief concern is with the spirit of the club. He wants the Vikings to play rough, to be 100 percent "physical," to hit hard, tackle hard, and run with the intent of banging right through any opposition. As a result, he produces a pass rush, for instance, that is about as devastating as anyone ever stood up against— four guys who act as if they were ready to blast their way through a brick wall to get at the quarterback.

Joe Schmidt has a similar philosophy. His boys may not

learn too much technique from Joe. But they do become infected with the same kind of ferocity Joe himself displayed when he was backing up the Detroit line. The Lions have long been known as a rough, tough club who are out to sting the enemy on every play. There is no letting down against the Lions, because they don't believe in letting down themselves. That is one reason I believe the Lions have been able to knock off some of the best-rated clubs in the league.

But no coach alive has ever invented a substitute for winning. A winning club, with the Superbowl and the other top prizes in view, will play its heart out for anyone. And a winning coach is always the greatest guy alive, no matter how repellent a personality he may carry around. Sometimes a club will unite around a quarterback and give out that extra effort that is always required to keep on winning. Sometimes it will be inspired by the coach. But if a team scores some upset victories against tough opposition, it will seem to grow stronger all by itself. That is because the game of football requires so much emotion. Men will outdo themselves only under the stress of strong emotion and unless a club really outdoes itself on the field on several critical occasions, it cannot reach the top.

I think Lombardi pointed out once that practically every coach in the business can think up sound plays and effective defenses. But bringing the club to the proper emotional pitch is the important job. Lombardi managed it. Sid Gilman can do it. George Allen specializes in it. Undoubtedly other coaches have concentrated on it too. And many times the emotion has been spontaneous, the result of an injury to a quarterback or other key player, or the sudden eruption of what the players call "pride"—in the team or in its current leader—and a frantic determination not to see it or him humiliated.

When a team finds itself out of the race, morale often collapses, and nothing but this mysterious "pride" will establish it again. There have been clubs that began to take special satisfaction in knocking off the contenders, even when they themselves were outdistanced. I think every athlete has in him somewhere this urge to knock the top dog off his stool and some coaches have been able to play on that urge successfully.

Many coaches have worked hard to cook up methods for getting a club "up" for a game. In college, it used to be fairly easy to play up some ancient rivalry to charge a squad up to the point where they were ready to shed blood. In the pros, you have to find some more substantial cause to fight for. Most squads will put out a little extra if they learn that they will be on national television. Now and then a coach will be able to stir his gang into a rage on the basis of some news story that belittles them. Once in a while, if a team is going to play in New York, you will find the guys especially eager to impress the big city crowd, to prove that San Diego doesn't have to take a back seat to the Metropolis. Sometimes there will be a carry-over of a grudge from season to season, because of some late hitting or a fist fight that was never settled.

More than one club used to go to Minnesota to face the Vikings, when Van Brocklin had them, with a real determination to draw blood. I am sure we will go back to New Orleans with that same feeling. The Forty-Niners and the Rams have about played their sectional rivalry to death, but there may be a little mileage in it still. The club that gets beaten in the Superbowl usually longs for another crack at the bunch that beat them, and will come up to the rematch with the juices flowing. But beyond that, the rivalries have to be artificially induced. George Allen tries to stir up his crowd with slogans and appeals to their pride. The Colts' management tried to induce some anger against Don Shula's Dolphins because Shula had presumably done Baltimore dirt. Paul Brown was able to inject into the Bengals his own desire to get even with the management of the Browns, who had "retired" him against his will a few years earlier.

Still, the chance for big money and the security it represents (by way of establishing a guy's reputation and spreading his fame) is what really inspires a professional football player. When that evaporates, it is hard to get a team "up" again. I know that in 1970 after our loss to Cincinnati, which put the play-offs out of reach, there was a sudden letting-down that you could almost feel. One or two of the best guys began to dodge practice on some excuse. Other guys just did not put out with their previous vigor. And the coach, Charley Waller, simply could not find the key to remotivating the squad. I am not sure anyone could have. A few of us still felt inwardly charged up, just for a chance to prove our rights to the job. But the strong unity, the sense of belonging to a group that was more important than any individual member, had begun to evaporate.

One factor in this letdown may have been the coach's own uncertainty about his future. I am sure he must have put in many hours of trying to justify his decisions, for he often seemed uncertain of what he had told us to do, and occasionally contradicted himself. I don't think a coach should ever have to find himself in a spot like this, because his own insecurity is too easily transmitted to the squad. The solution, I suppose, is for the club owners to give a coach full charge, provide him with a piece of the action as incentive, and then stick with him through storm and calm.

I have an idea the coaches' union would go for that plan too. But whether it could be implemented without dampening a lot of interest on the part of the owners is something I am not smart enough to work out.

The coach is supposed to prepare his charges mentally as well as physically for the battle, and to keep their emotions at the proper pitch. But it sometimes happens that his own emotions get away from him. There have been games at which the opposing quarterbacks have been forty degrees cooler than their coaches.

Several times over the past two seasons I have known some coach to swallow the apple under extreme tension, when the guys on his team were still crisp as fresh crackers. At Green Bay one time, Phil Bengston sent Don Horn into a game after Bart Starr had hurt his arm and urged Don to stay cool, inasmuch as *all* the plays would be sent in from the sideline. So Don took over, called the first play the coach had given him, and made two yards. In came another play. This one gained four yards. It was third down, four yards to go. What do we do now, coach? Don stood in the huddle staring at the sideline. No one was moving his way. Bengston kept his eyes averted. The referee began to growl: "Get out of the huddle!"

So Don called time and moved toward the sideline. At this Bengston came to life.

"What's the matter with you?" he yelled. "Don't you know the game plan? Couldn't you think of *something?*" So Don thought of something but the club blew the game.

It is this sort of thing that makes so many of the guys respect Paul Brown. He *never* lets his quarterback take the heat, even on the occasions (it sometimes happens) that he sends a messenger in without any play, just to keep the opposition guessing. If anything goes wrong on Brown's club, it's the coach's fault and he stands up and says so.

In our 1970 game with Denver here in San Diego we won by running out the clock in the last few seconds, when they could have beaten us by a field goal. The Broncos would have stopped us and taken the ball but for a pass-interference call. At that call, Lou Saban blew his stack as fiercely as ever I have seen a sane man do. He ran up and down the sidelines like a wild dog on a chain, hysterical with rage, and screaming at the officials until I thought he'd pop a vein in his neck. When the gun went off, he actually sprinted after the officials, intending God knows what degree of mayhem. Fortunately, a couple of his own guys grabbed him and held him until he stopped frothing.

That same season I saw both coaches in a game lose control both of themselves and of the teams. We were playing in Oakland and I must say that Charley Waller had plenty of provocation, for this was the game I have already told about when one official overruled another and robbed us of a chance to win. From the moment of that call, Charley took off into the upper atmosphere, yelling imprecations, gesturing wildly, running up and down the line, in such a state that he lost all track of what was going on on the field and so failed to make the adjustments he might have made that could have saved us some little hope. But the rival coach, John Madden, meanwhile flew into a wild orbit of his own and for a long time the two clubs went their own way as if they had both been suddenly orphaned by the same lightning bolt.

It may well be that they both felt extreme pressure from the fact that in both cases there was a sort of Supercoach in the background, either calling the shots himself or openly wishing he could. Everyone knows that Al Davis is the real boss at Oakland and that he second-guesses his coach continually. So the man on the field can be expected to act as if he were standing barefooted on a hot griddle, because that's just what he *is* doing.

The situation on the San Diego side was not exactly the same. Sid Gilman sat up in the press box and talked to me on the phones. He did a hell of a good job too, in analyzing mistakes, spotting weaknesses, and suggesting plays. It is too bad he could not divide himself in two and work the upstairs position as well as the place on the sidelines. But that was impossible, so Charley had to make the major decisions and always had to weigh Sid's suggestions against his own ideas. Usually he called it Sid's way. But he surely must have been conscious of those sharp eyes upstairs. And I am positive he was torn between wanting to be his own man and desiring to follow the advice of the boss who had his deep respect.

So here were Madden and Waller, trying to outsmart each other on the sidelines, trying to anticipate each other's moves, trying to guess what the boss might be thinking, and all the while reacting to the tension of a fiercely fought game that was not decided until the final seconds.

As a matter of fact, I wonder why more coaches do not go half bananas in a crucial game, because the job has been made nearly impossible by certain tired traditions that are left over from a more innocent era.

The notion of the coach as dictator—not only of his team's moves on the field but of their off-the-field behavior, their sleeping schedule, and their conditioning programs—should have gone out with the retirement of George Halas. Many of the rules a coach and his staff have to enforce and a lot of the haranguing they feel constrained to go in for are aimless, unnecessary, and futile.

To stay in proper condition, men do need a regimen of

some sort. And, as I said, it is just about impossible for a man to impose this on himself for any extended period. All the same, the rules ought to have some relation to reality. The "bedtime" for most football players is ridiculously early, better suited to a gang of high school kids. As a matter of fact, to ask a quarterback to go to sleep at half-past eleven o'clock the night before an important game is like ordering the sun to rise an hour later—it's against nature.

I well recall the Saturday night before the Jet game, when John Hadl and I stayed awake until almost dawn, trying in vain to sleep, then sitting up to talk about the game, to send down for countless Cokes and shrimp cock-tails, to try to relax by watching the late shows on TV. It should be noted that John gave one of his greatest perform-ances next day. I think it was useful for him to loosen up and artificial efforts to force sleep upon us would have just added to the tension. Of course, a whole string of 4 a.m. bedtimes would have begun to tell on our condition. But the night before a game—especially a crucial game— is bound to bring taut nerves that take extra time to loosen up.

Most adult athletes react well to a rather easy rein. And most bedtime hours are too damned early anyway. When a man's "work day" begins about noon and ends at five, there is no reason why he cannot safely stay awake until well past midnight.

There may be special cases where some particular player requires extra rest. But all players are not the same and the best coaches adjust their methods to the individual, tightening the rein on the guys that need it, and making no pretense of doing otherwise. A coach who explains his methods straightforwardly and treats his men like equals earns the respect of the squad. And men are quick to obey the rules of a man they respect.

It also seems to be a coaching tradition to stop practice now and then to ream out a player, yell a lot of advice and exhortation, and go in for several minutes of plain bull-shitting about almost anything from the National Guard (which Charley Waller once insisted was interfering with my performance) to chances of making the play-offs. If the bullshit were removed from practice, if players were corrected in private, or called aside after practice, and if the work were better organized, it would be possible to run off twice as many plays in skeleton drill as we run now.

We have two assistant coaches—both, as it happens, from the South—who enjoy unusual rapport with the players, chiefly because they habitually "tell it like it is." Bum Phillips is perhaps the most popular. He is a guy who will tell a player: "You give 100 percent all right. But you just don't have that much talent!" But he will also listen to the players and invite their comments. He is about the only coach I know of who will frequently say to a player: "What do you think?" And there is never any doubt about what *he* thinks.

Jackie Simpson, who coaches the defensive secondary, has the happiest crowd on the field. His charges are all black and the blacks are particularly attracted to a guy who speaks his mind openly and plays fair. None of them ever has any doubts about Jackie's opinion of their efforts. And they know that when Jackie says he is going to do something, he'll do it just the way he said. Both these guys agree that you can only coach a man so much, that by the time a man reaches the pros, his basic talents are all developed and that you can't turn a natural slowpoke into an All-Pro by yelling at him.

It is important too that the coach enjoy football and not tackle it as if he were trying to make a bunch of draftees ready for a last-ditch battle. The men who work for Paul Brown all come away with the conviction that the Old Man likes the game and enjoys every second of it. That may be the basic secret of his ability to develop a crowd of youngsters into pro contenders in record time. Practice is not always going to be 100 percent "fun." But it would become far less wearing and monotonous if the same play was not repeated and repeated in the same afternoon, so that football began to seem like working the assembly line. It seems plain enough that people learn faster and hold on to their lessons longer when the learning process is in itself enjoyable. The enjoyment in athletics comes from a sense of accomplishment, which monotonous drill can eventually stifle.

8

This Is the Life

If there is brutality in a pro football player's life—and who can deny it?—it's not really pervasive. There is always a chance of someone's being racked up, but it does not happen often and no one can play good football if he keeps that possibility on his mind. The spearing, the hitting, the sparring, the belting take place but once a week, and if you are big and strong and healthy you can take them and even enjoy them, the way most healthy young animals enjoy mock combat with no hard feelings and no desire to kill.

The rest of the week has special graces that make most guys glad they are working at this trade and not fitting nuts on bolts, drawing lines on paper, climbing poles, or trying to talk someone into buying something. Once the summer practice, with its exhausting two-a-day drill sessions is over, the hard work is reserved for Sunday. During the week, there is much studying of films and attending class, and work on offense and defense. But there is no hard hitting, no scrimmaging, no hand-to-hand battling.

Monday is an off day. Tuesday the "work" begins with a quarterback meeting at 10:00 a.m. I start out from my apartment in Point Loma for the 17-mile drive to the stadium, with stops at the post office and at the bank, where I gather up loot enough to last me the week. The drive is as routine to me as to any commuter—just a day at the office, only my office is outdoors. Sometimes I stop at the publicity office and pick up photographs enough to take care of my autograph requests, sign them and mail them.

Then I check in to our meeting to go over, with John Hadl and the coaches, the lessons we learned on Sunday.

There is skeleton drill during the day—passers and receivers working (without contact) against the defensive backfield. This past season I got relatively little chance to pass in these drills once the regular season began, so that I used to look forward to Sunday when I would get an opportunity to heave some long spirals during warm-ups and imagine myself completing the bombs to Lance or to Gary or to Willie Frazier that would put us in the Superbowl.

During the week, once we have the films of the club we are going to meet the following Sunday, we run offensive plays against enemy defenses, then run their plays against our defenses. We also run, in skeleton form, once the game plan has been worked out, the plays that we have decided (from study of the films, and from our knowledge of our own personnel) may be successful against this club.

There is nothing brutal or dangerous about any of this work. The guys starting at noon warm up by playing catch with the football, trotting here and there on the field and testing out strained muscles and doubtful joints. Then they do a dozen or so "forties" (40-yard sprints) at good speed and use the calisthenic period to catch their breath. There are individual drills on techniques—centers practice spiraling balls back to the kicker, kickers kick, linemen work out "moves," and running backs take hand-offs.

The quarterbacks, meanwhile, working with center and receivers, throw various patterns against the linebackers and safeties. There is a team drill, without tackling, in which our offense tests "their" defense. We practice goalline plays, again without tackling, and we test our defense against "their" offense. The kickoff, punt return, and kicking teams have a session of their own and the workout closes with more "forties" by everyone except those whose injuries keep them from running. The day ends about 5:00 p.m. with a shower.

The quarterbacks meet again in the evening—and that's *our* work day. If the club has been winning, it can be exhilarating, if sometimes a bit monotonous. If we have been losing it can be a pain in the ass—but only a slight one.

The locker room is always alive, a little rowdier than a college locker room, with rougher language and rougher practical jokes. Willie Frazier may bring a snake into the room and hide him somewhere to startle a teammate. Once he dropped one into the tube that held the rolls of adhesive, then asked Andy Rice to fetch him some tape. Andy picked up the tube and shook it to dislodge the last roll. A busy little garter snake dropped squirming into his palm and Andy, who has a naturally high-pitched voice, let out a "Holy Jesus Christ!" that sounded like a blast from a steam whistle. Willie, of course, broke up.

Willie has a natural gift for capturing small animals and is likely to have something alive in his room all the time. Once he spotted a small hawk on the grass and tossed a blanket over it. He put it in his room and amused himself by sending people up to his door on various errands. When the door opened, the hawk would explode in a racket of wild wings and flying feathers, scaring the living shit out of the visitor. Happily, the guy who owned the hawk reclaimed it before Willie had time to build it a new home.

Once I had the bad manners to open my mouth in a tremendous yawn during a team meeting, and Willie, who was sitting right behind me and must have been tensely waiting for the moment, popped a few Mexican peppers into my mouth then clapped his hand over it (he is stronger than Ajax, believe me) and held tight until I had to swallow the damn things or die. I nearly died anyway. Burn? I thought he had stuffed a lighted packet of matches down my throat. It was hours before my mouth and throat returned to normal. And Willie took a fit of hysterics every time he looked at me.

Mostly our good times are a little less juvenile than this. Football players generally are good-natured, outgoing people who make pleasant companions. Some day I may weary of the plane trips we take and tire of motel life and seeking out eating and drinking spots in strange cities. Several of the married guys find the long trips a drag. Not me. I am still yokel enough to relish the opportunity to sniff out the

fun places in unfamiliar cities. The travel to me is a good
part of the joy of football.

Not that there isn't fun to be had at home. Not many
people lead a pleasanter life than mine, with my Point
Loma apartment just a long jump from the beach, where
you can run, or bicycle, or swim, or lie in the sun in the
flawless California weather. When we play our game at
home, we spend Saturday night all together at the Hilton
Inn on Mission Bay and usually have our pre-game meal
on Saturday at Pericano's, an Italian restaurant where there
is no drink but wine (you have to ask for water) and
where the boss allows no salt, pepper, or other condiments
on the table. *He* flavors the food! Ah, that deep-fried
zucchini!

We fly to our out-of-town games in chartered planes, an
aspect of the job that really troubles a few of the players,
including John Hadl. Ever since those college-team
crashes, there has been more open nervousness on our
club as the plane takes to the air. The club, in one voice,
urges the pilot to get the plane aloft: "Get it up, Bussy!
(all drivers are 'bussy'—for bus-driver) Get it up! Come on,
Bussy! Get it up! Ahhhhh! We're up!"

John never fails to flinch as the landing gear *(chunk!
chunk!)* folds into retracted position. And I take special
care to remind him when we are flying over open water:
"What a spot to come down in, John! You could probably
swim to shore from here, couldn't you?" This brings bad
words from John. But there is sweat on his face and hands.

Almost every city has its special pleasures. The first job
always is to find the spot where the girls are, even though
we often arrive on a Friday night too late for much prowling. The family men hit the sack but we bachelors sample
the drinks and "atmosphere" of whatever drinking spots
we can find to reckon the percentages—the chances of making out with some unclaimed lovely.

The next job is to locate the best eating place in town.
Here we O.D. on the local specialty—seafood, roast beef,
steak, tacos, veal parmigiana, or whatever—in midafter-
noon on Saturday. The night meal on Saturday, the pre-

game meal, is a relatively light one, and we go on the field
next day feeling hungry.

After the game there is no time for touring the night
spots. The whole squad tumbles off the bus at the airport
and races for the bar, to inhale whatever beers we can
work in before boarding time. Occasionally there are minutes enough for some of the quick drinkers to attain a
state of bliss before we are airborne. And if we have won
the game, there may be champagne aboard, with lots of
merriment. The brass—and the sports writers—sit in the
first-class section while the players, and sometimes a few
of the assistant coaches, sit in the rear. We have two or
three players who make it a point now always to get as
far back in the plane as they can go, on the theory I
suppose that if there is a crash, the rear end may escape
some of the impact. As for me, I sometimes wonder why
the hell the sportswriters get choice accommodations while
there are assistant coaches who have to take back seats.

Of all the cities we go to, New York of course is
the best for me. It is my native turf in a way and I
know where the food is best and where fun and females
abound. The "percentages" are high here, not only in the
singles joints along Second Avenue but in all the midtown
late spots. And the chow hounds find menus to suit every
whim.

Cincinnati and Cleveland, however, are no places for a
horny young out-of-town bachelor to improve his average.
The spot to go in Cincinnati is supposed to be the Playboy
Club. All I can say is that it is exactly what it sounds
like—the Playboy Club in Cincinnati. There are probably
family-type restaurants in this town made attractive by
their old-time German flavor. But in the hip joints there
seems to be a kind of pathetic and unsuccessful effort to
imitate the swinging atmosphere of a New York bar.

Cleveland too is a great place to encourage celibacy. It
is, we found, more fun than Wooster. But all the atmosphere has kind of a minor league quality, an imitation of
the Eastern cities with no character of its own. This to us
was a "room service" town, for we never found a really
great place to eat.

Denver is my first choice next to New York. Everything about this city seems alive and young and swinging. The crisp clean air, always with a smell of snow, the infusion of gangs of kids from the nearby colleges, the free-and-easy air in bars and restaurants—they make me sorry to go away and eager to get back. You feel healthier just walking the streets there and looking out your motel window at the Rocky Mountain scenery. Unattached and pretty girls are numerous at the bars and there is always the feeling that there is plenty of room and that you are bound to be welcome wherever you find yourself.

No one raised much hell in Denver on our last trip there. With the help of a filling-station proprietor we found a little log-cabin restaurant where well-fed cowboy types, in wide hats and bulging britches, took up much of the room and where we found the coldest beer in the west, along with great kielbase (Polish sausage) sandwiches. It was awe-inspiring to see how much beer those local folk could siphon down. The recreation here was those bar-room board games—shuffle board and bowling. Mike Mercer, who must have wasted much of his youth in saloons like this, proved a whiz at the games, a real pro who picked up all the bets.

Of course Chicago is New York all over again, with a strip where you can find a singles bar on every corner and some in between. This, like New York, is a "high potential" town, as far as girls go. There are stewardesses by the plane-load—at Mother's, at the Green Onion, and one or two more. It may be that Chicago looked especially good to me because we won our game there and because I beat Dick Butkus on a quarterback draw that gained us eleven yards.

Winners always have more fun than losers and this win was satisfying to both John Hadl and me. Especially satisfying to me because I carried the ball on the play that beat Butkus, and did it twice. The first time, it was fourth and about a yard and a half to go on Chicago's 24. The coach sent in an off-tackle play to pick up the first down. At the snap, Butkus, who seems to have second sight at times, reacted perfectly. He stunted to the strong side and was exactly where he needed to be to stop that play dead. But the pulling guard had lined up a shade too deep and when he moved to lead the play he knocked the ball out of my hands before I could give it off.

Everybody went through the play and the defense moved to meet the thrust. But the ball had struck the ground and bounced straight up so that I recovered it at once. There was a big hole right ahead of me. I squeezed the ball tight and shot through for the first down and a little more. Butkus could not believe he had been wrong.

"Jesus Christ!" he bellowed. "You lucky son of a bitch!"

In the next series, we had the ball on their twelve-yard line, when I called a quarterback draw. This time old Dick fell for the fake and began to drop off on pass coverage. He half turned his head to look into his secondary to check on the coverage, and as he did I skipped right past him. I was gone before he realized I had the ball. I made it to the one-yard line, and we scored immediately afterward. I just *loved* Chicago after that.

Kansas City is probably not everyone's favorite town but it is one of mine because a combination of happy circumstances provides it with choice food and choice girls. There is a school for stewardesses there, so that we are afforded the opportunity of completing the girls' training in bump-and-run and other techniques. The best food, for my taste, is not at the steak houses but at the Taco Shop where they certainly serve the *greatest* tacos north of the border and where the beer is cold, cold, *cold*.

Los Angeles is a depressing place to me, not only because of the smog but because it sprawls so that you seem to spend most of your off-time driving. An evening there is so full of freeways and zooming traffic that you are half-pooped out before the fun ever begins. The Sport Page cocktail lounge is full of really nice girls and often has live music, if you have any strength left to enjoy them. The eating place most of us choose is Matteo's, which seems crowded with celebrities but in spite of the fact has good Italian food.

Most of us expected to find New Orleans the most swinging town on the circuit, with Bourbon Street running over with old-world glamour and old-time jazz. Instead we found a sort of carnival town with a lot of hole-in-the-wall spots that are not unlike what you might find along 42nd Street in New York—topless go-go girls, heavy smoke, mediocre food and drink, although here and there you could O. D. on really fine shrimp. Al Hirt's was probably the best restaurant we struck, with prices that would make your flesh crawl. But of course our prowling time was limited.

What amazed me most about New Orleans was that it seemed surrounded by nearly endless swamps, with a great old house standing sometimes all alone in a swamp so dreary and wide that you would wonder how men and women could bear to stay there.

The black players were more at home in New Orleans than in any other Southern city, far more than in Miami, for instance, where most of them were especially uneasy. In New Orleans there seemed to be many more black people on hand and more places where a black man could go without embarrassment. As for Houston, it may be that place looked especially depressing to me because we played there on Thanksgiving Day, still aching a little from the Sunday game. It is a muggy, sprawling city—just no place to go for relaxation, and a city where the black players made sure their friends met them at the airport and hustled them off to civilization.

Most of us had never seen the Astrodome before, so we anticipated a thrill there, and were not disappointed. In every way it seems the ideal spot to play or to watch football, or any outdoor game. Even the Astroturf seems flawless, because it gives good footing, with no bare or greasy spots or puddles. Once you come down hard on it, however, as I did, you realize why the players would rather have grass. It has a backing of something as hard as asphalt that has, I believe, provided more fractures than any other playing surface. It sure as hell knocked the sense out of me when I hit it head first. And it can *burn* your hide.

Maybe Miami is the Fun Capital of the Universe but I am not able to cast a vote on that. We stayed at Fort Lauderdale and had to hop to Miami, five to a cab for

twenty miles. There was talk of the delights we might
wallow in at the Wreck Bar or the Post and Paddock but
the thought of that cab ride so damaged my appetite that I
settled for a home-grown hamburger. Besides, who can be
truly comfortable in a city where your black teammates are
made to feel as if they had walked into the dining room
with their pants unzipped? Anyway, it was hot as hell
there, as in all the Southern cities our schedule carried us
to.

You have to understand that a football team, or at least
our football team, seeks its fun together. Perhaps a third
of the club, being family men and church-goers, spend
their late evening hours curled up with the *Wall Street
Journal* or hanging on the long-distance phone. But the
bachelor contingent, black and white, usually go looking
for fun together. (In Houston, and other Southern cities,
the blacks sought out local friends.) We expect to find
conditions everywhere as they are in California, where
there is no craning of the neck and muttering, no indignant
or unbelieving stares, no glowering visages at the sight of
a black man and a white girl enjoying each other's company. Any place that sets out to bar blacks, in the manner
of the unreconstructed South, might just as well put up a
sign that closes the place to pro football players altogether.

In spite of the fact that we played in Boston on the
dreariest day of the year, with cold rain and mud and a
clammy breath off the river, and despite our loss of three
hours en route, which forced us to finish dinner in almost
a dead heat with the curfew, Boston is still one of the
cities I would rather be in.

During the overlong (six-hour) flight to Boston, everyone had worked out what he figured was his private blue-
print for an attack upon the fun spots. The Eastern natives
had lined up their excitement through old college pals and
one-time girl friends, and were ready to take immediate
aim on one of their standard haunts—Joe Namath's Bachelors III, Cappelletti's Extra Point, or some less noted fill-
ing station. Addresses of all such shops were eagerly passed
around on the plane, so no time need be wasted after landing. There being exactly three hours available for Rest and

Rehabilitation between ETA and bed-check, we wanted nothing to stay us in our beeline trip to a warm meal and cold drinks. Because the time was so short, nobody really envisioned anything more elaborate—although nobody was going to turn down the bonus of liquid eyes and warm breasts should they be promptly available.

There were five of us in the cab that shot out of Logan airport minutes after the Charger plane touched down— Gary Garrison, Walt Sweeney, Rick Redman, Steve De-Long and me. Our target was Bachelors III, managed by Tad Dowdy, a partner of Joe the Jet. Tad greeted us at the door to the dim and smoke-filled den, already packed tight in honor of Friday night. But Tad rushed us in and found us a table at once on the basis of a "reservation" that had just occurred to him. We gulped a drink, ordered steak sandwiches, had a more leisurely drink, and began to appraise the local lovelies. Was it the dim lights, the press of time, the strong drink, or is it true that Boston girls are prettier even than the belles of the South? We thought so as we sat munching our sandwiches and cursing the stupid curfew. We were three hours behind the Boston time, so we felt entilted to stretch the evening a little bit. Another drink or two and curfew was right upon us, just time to crawl into a cab and scoot back across the river to our motel before bed-check. Everyone made it on time and when the chosen hour struck every little Charger was snuggled safe in his bed—or so the coaches believed. Actually, we just could not adjust to the time change. Sitting with our shoes off, Jake (a made-up name for my companion) and I had just exchanged a few gripes when we heard a dull bump as the fire-escape door on our corridor opened and closed—once, twice, three times. My God, it was a mass break! With hardly a word spoken we jumped off of our beds at the same instant and pulled on our shoes. Jake called Tad to check the current height of activity back there, learned that the Muzak still played and the wine still flowed, and motioned me to follow. On tiptoe we trotted to the fire escape and before the bell in the Old North Church, or anywhere else, had struck one a.m., we were in a cab on our way back to Park Square.

At Bachelors III all was dim, stifling, noisy, and delight-
ful, exactly as if we had never been away. With no scowl-
ing clock to dull our pleasures or cut them down in their
prime, Jake and I lay back and paid even closer heed to
all the mini-skirted lovelies who adorned the background.
Jake drank a cocktail and ate a bowl of chili. I sent several scotches down after those that had visited me before.
Tad came to sit with us and to answer our questions on the
probable response of this one or that one among his female
help to an indecent proposition. As we toyed with the
fantasies this discussion evoked, Jake suddenly gripped my
arm and went rigid.

"Let's," he gasped, "get the fuck out of here! Willie just
walked in!" (Willie—not his real name—being one of the
assistant coaches into whose care the boss had commended
our morals, Jake's suggestion made excellent sense.) Tad,
with the instincts of an experienced late-spot proprietor,
immediately sprinted for the entrance, to lay roadblocks
in Willie's path. Then he returned to guide us out the
backdoor and accept our earnest thank-you's. Willie could
not possibly have spotted us, we assured each other, what
with the smoke and the dim lights and all (but we had
known Willie!). Anyway, I offered, Willie is a hot shit himself and would never turn us in. Thus comforted, we
returned to the motel, or almost to the motel. We had the
cabby stop a block away and we walked the final few
rods, solemnly praying to each other that "the fucking back
door is still open."

The back door is open and we move almost without
sound up the fire-stairs. At our landing, Jake pulls the
door open just enough for him to protrude his skull into a
corridor and check for coaches. All clear. Softly as thieves,
we file down the carpeted hall, then scramble for the door
like two young brothers just in from their first might of
drinking strong liquor. Jake begins to snicker and I find
myself laughing aloud as he tries madly to fit the key into
the doorlock.

Then my God there is the sound of the elevator at our
floor! A coach? It is *bound* to be. And this could cost us
a thousand apiece! We both hold our breath as the elevator

door slides open and Jake gives the key one final frantic twist. The door does not yield and we both turn to stare into the eyes of our merry teammate Walt Sweeney, who has swaggered right into the elevator to make *his* way to bed. Walt stops and glares at us with make-believe indignation.

"What you guys up to?" he demands. "Breaking the fuckin' curfew?" Whereupon he takes a sudden fit of laughing. Jake and I laugh too. The key slides home, the door opens, and we go happily to bed, to sleep deeply and sweetly until next forenoon.

Our Saturday glutton party was held in mid-afternoon at Pier Four, where the sea-food must be the best ever caught and cooked. And we all blessed Boston. So friendly, so close together, no need to buck traffic half the night. We won the game too and even enjoyed most of the long flight home, during which a few of the guys could not stop declaiming on the joys of the city we were leaving. (Those, some cynic snarled, are the guys who got laid.)

One of the aspects that made Boston most attractive to me was our staying in Cambridge, on Memorial Drive, with the air of Harvard all about us. The Ivy League atmosphere, indeed any college atmosphere, always affects me with deep nostalgia and sets me to fantasizing about the days when perhaps I can return to it—for law studies? And advanced degree in anthropology? Who knows?

A few of the players were turned off at the extremes of long hair and hippy dress affected by some of the students. "Can you *believe* that?" they would ask each other, just as they used to at summer camp at Irvine when some college youngster in the beer joint would utter an anti-Establishment blasphemy. To the white veterans and the coaches long hair is synonymous with Communism, such is the extent of their political sophistication. John Hadl, whose own college days belong to a previous decade, could not stop shaking his head at some of the "weirdos" who crossed Harvard Yard.

I assured John that even the Kansas University campus, where he was once a hero, now looked like this. He shook his head some more. All the same, he hopes to send his own son to Harvard when he is grown. And I would not mind, after the football wars are over, settling myself in here for several quiet semesters.

Almost the opposite of Boston in our experience had been Houston, where we lighted, as I said, two days before Thanksgiving in my rookie year, when just the act of flying anywhere as a member of a pro football club still set tiny thrills to skipping through my bones. Houston was hotter than the Devil's Graveyard. And our coming there in midweek, after a game on Sunday, had us all cursing the dumb-ass bastard who had made the schedule. Our bones still aching and we had to play *another* game?

I was privately agog to see the Astrodome and it did not disappoint me—that green, windless, mudless, glareless paradise!

The arrival in Houston saw no scrambling after cabs and checking of addresses and local phone numbers. Only the black players had taken care to have friends on hand to spirit them away. The rest of us straggled to our rooms to savor our victory over Denver and to rest our bones. We arrived early in the day, yet no one at first seemed to harbor any plans for other recreation than sleep and gorging himself.

But as the darkness grew deeper, there was a general re-igniting of the itch to test the local temptations. We bachelor types began to gather in one room or another to exchange addresses of body shops and discuss prospects.

My own interest is but a flicker, for I am eager to post my second good game in a row. I am still more tired than normal and would happily settle for several cold beers. Anyway it's *Tuesday*. What the hell could be happening at a bar on Tuesday?

Nevertheless, we finally set out in a group for the recommended discotheque (name now happily forgotten) where what to our wondering eyes should appear but a group of Texas girls in cowgirl costume. In their own odd way they are unusually appealing. Is there some genetic factor that always juxtaposes a Deep South accent with generous breasts? These girls, it rapidly turns out, are especially attracted to physical types like pro football players and it takes very little parleying indeed to persuade them that there is more to life than sipping small cold drinks and hearing records over and over—and that, whatever it is, it is to be found back in our rooms at the hotel.

What goddamned nonsense we go through to get them there! Even looking back on it almost two years later I feel twinges of embarrassment. We ask the girls to wait a few minutes outside the hotel, while we find our way to the suite where our fun is centered. Then they are to follow, hop in an elevator, go to the floor above ours, and walk down! Did we really imagine we were deceiving anyone by this corny maneuver? Well, at least we escape the glittering eye of the coach and get to the rooms. Within minutes the girls are there. Now we hasten to bring room service hotfooting on high, bearing booze, with which we hope to complete this mass seduction. The booze arrives, the glasses clink, the girls and boys grow cozy—and then, for God's sake, there is a sharp knock on the door!

A coach? A teammate? Either one is bad news. A coach means the end of the party. A teammate, unless he has a girl in tow, is simply going to try to move in on *our* action. And there is just enough to go around. We open the door a crack and it is shoved the rest of the way. It is good old George (an alias) with his eyes aglitter. No use to try to bar the door to him, for if we did not invite him in, jolting George would soon have the door off its hinges.

George zeroes in first on the booze and when he has partaken of that, he carefully appraises the females. Not that he is in any state to be particular. Being, to use the local vernacular, half shit-faced already, George would be a menace to any female under 85. One guy, reading the signs, takes his girl by the hand and slips out to return to his own room. But my room is occupied by John Hadl, now deep in sleep or else poring over playbooks. So I have no corner to hide in. Neither has Bill, whose room this is. And George has fastened his eye on Bill's girl.

A veteran of such encounters and so far gone now in

beer and booze that he feels no restraint of friendship or
common courtesy, George has drawn close to Bill's young
lady and starts to explain in specific terms what he has
in mind for the immediate moment. Bill tries to ease his
girl away. Both girls grow more and more nervous at the
ripeness of George's language and have begun to eye the
door. As Bill extends his efforts to draw his girl beyond
George's reach, George grows ugly and urges Bill to lay
off or experience a quick rap on the mouth. Bill is ready
for *that* deal and it seems for a moment as if it will be
George and Bill all over the hotel floor. The girls are
openly alarmed now and George begins to shout at
them. Now they both start for the door and George,
suddenly repentant, urges them to stay.

"I'll go!" he promises. "It's all my fault! I'll get the
hell out of here! You girls stay here and have fun!"

But it is much too late to mollify the ladies and one of
them in her genteel southern tones invites George to "go
play with youahself somewheah!"

At this, George becomes really pissed. He leaps to his
feet, grabs a beer bottle by the throat and yells: "I'll give
you broads five seconds to get the fuck out of here or
I'll brain you both!"

The girls need no hand to urge them. Swift as two
little mink, they scoot out the door. As the door closes
behind them, George punctuates their departure by heaving
the bottle. Crash! The bottle disintegrates harmlessly. Bill
and George and I now look at each other and suddenly
we begin to laugh. We have to sit down then and laugh
and laugh, until we find the strength to go to bed—drunk,
weary, and wondering what the hell we almost got into.

We won the game 17 to 10. But somehow I seldom
feel a yen any more to go back to Houston. All of us
bachelors were happy to board the plane for home, to dip
our tired beaks in the cold beer that awaited us, and to
grin foolishly when we met each other's eyes.

It is on the trips that the world of pro football seems
most like Never-Never Land. If we win the Sunday game,
the fun is unremitting, and even if we lose there are the
Friday and Saturday before the game when life tastes good

all over. The plane rides are often filled with drink and laughter and gambling for the per diem dough (a ten-dollar bill and two ones). The black players introduced a card game called Tonk that I never learned to make sense of. But poker is played most and played for the highest stakes. John and I like to risk our per diem on Liars Poker, played by matching serial numbers on a dollar bill.

It is only at home that there is time for chewing at yourself over what you may do with your life when the arms and legs finally begin to calcify, and not too many of the players go in for that sort of brooding. The white players in pro football are generally pro-Establishment types, or are simply too out of touch with the real world to bother with any political thought except whatever is handed to them right off the racks.

It is here that our black brothers differ most radically; that may be one reason why I find their company more stimulating. Joe Beauchamp is our team Communist—not really a subversive but just called "the Communist" because of his often militant stand on the race question and his readiness to speak his mind. But there is no real bitterness between Joe and the white players. Typical of Joe is a remark he made one evening as we rode the bus home from the Saturday movie. (There is always a movie that the whole team attends the night before a game, to help us all relax and to preserve that "family" feeling.) The week before we had watched Marlon Brando in *Burned,* which deals largely with the brutalizing of rebellious blacks. This week it was Anthony Quinn in *Flap,* where the American Indian takes it up the ass in every reel. As we rode home in the bus, Joe yelled out above all the competing chatter: "When the hell we going to see *you* bastards get it? When we going to see *Custer's Last Stand?*"

Come to think of it, the matter of race equality is the one point on which the majority in pro football, the Establishment types, are at one with the hippies. On every other matter, the squares on the club look on the long-hairs as invaders from some small and noisome planet a hundred light-years off. At Irvine, the players and the college youths mingled, or at least crossed orbits, only at the nearby beer-joint, where it was possible to hear skinny youths denounce the Administration in tones loud enough to rattle the glassware. Most of the jocks, who had spent their own college years letting it all hang out for dear old Southwest Indiana State, found it hard to credit their senses. They would gape at the youths and at each other.

"If the little pricks ever want some place to burn down," some player was sure to growl, "I hope they start right here!"

There is unanimity on one aspect of Women's Lib, however. There is hardly a man on the squad who objects to the no-bra rule.

Still we don't have any really active rightist of the Jackie Kemp stripe. Jackie, they tell me, was 100 percent P.R.—talking to you without ever really hearing what you said. Under his influence the Players Association developed all the sturdy qualities of a company union. (Our crowd may dutifully vote for Ronald Reagan and Spiro Agnew. But they are all for collective bargaining and against the option clause.)

It is almost too easy, living a life so unbesmirched by personal woe, to forget that there are real troubles in that outer world we may all some day be dumped into. Now the guys may gripe mildly that the chances of laying up a little extra from endorsements and the like are so restricted here. Some may have reveries of being traded to where the Astroturf grows softer.

Pay in pro football is not really anybody's dream of avarice and I can imagine a small family's chewing its way through the average salary of a lineman without having to gulp. I think $22,000 would represent the average earnings of a pro offensive lineman, even on the best paid squad. Considering that ten years is a long career in such a position, this hardly qualifies a man for membership in the Plutocrat's Club. Running backs average closer to $30,000. But then their careers are often far shorter. Defensive linemen last longer, earn less than running backs but slightly more than offensive linemen—perhaps because their feats can be particularized more by the coaches and TV commentators. But even they seldom get past 14 years on the job—and that's a long time even for a quarterback, whose skills seem to deteriorate most slowly and who earns the largest salary, with wide receivers next in line. Receivers are relatively long-lived in the profession too. But how many are there who have been working more than twelve seasons?

Every baseball club nowadays has a player in the $100,000 range. Basketball players often earn far more. The football player who takes home a salary like that has to be a quarterback or running back with a "package" program of some sort that spreads his money over half his career. And there are not a dozen in the whole league.

One reason why almost all players hope to land in New York is for the opportunities there for higher outside income. Players who fill the obigatory speaking engagements in New York will pocket fees of a couple of hundred or more. In San Diego, we get $25 and a free meal.

There are of course a number of guys who have found part-time occupations for the off-season, or who have managed to trade their local reputations into a decent cash return. Dickie Post has made a success of his clothing shop. John Hadl has earned himself the use of a Datsun station wagon, plus $1000 cash and a handful of credit cards, through doing commercials. John also gets paid for putting in three hours a day watching and analyzing films of potential opponents in action. (Pro football players, and particularly quarterbacks, as well as coaches, spend an inordinate amount of time at the movies—game movies, that is. For instance, before we met the New York Giants in 1970 pre-season, I watched films of the Giants in action no less than ten times. And one time, there was instant and total involvement by all coaches and players when some free soul slipped a spool of stag-reel on the projection machine. The "mistake" was corrected after the reel was run through.)

Lance Alworth gathers a little random bread through allowing his picture to be displayed on billboards to advertise the Allen John stores. But most of the endorsement income goes to Superbowl heroes or members of the New York teams. I have to confess, however, that I am not really aflame with envy at this because my better nature always itches mildly at the petty swindle of pretending to eat, smoke, drink, or wear something I would not consume unless they paid me to.

If a man does not make the grade with a pro club and is not traded off or claimed on waivers he may wind up on the cab squad (so-called because Mickey McBride, who invented the Cleveland Browns, was a taxicab magnate who set his reserves to driving taxis). Pay here is poor but may be supplemented by weekly stipends for playing in the Continental League, where a quarterback may earn as much as $1000 a game but where most players do well to collect $125, the kind of money that was paid linemen in the National League forty years ago. The Continental League does not feed players into the National League to the degree that the baseball minors feed them into the majors. A few players start out there but most are sent to the Continental while on the taxi squad of a big club, or they wind up there when nobody in the big league or in Canada can use them.

There are about twenty guys who spend the whole year in San Diego. The vested players—that is, those who are assured of the moderate pension that the Players' Association agreement has established—usually do no more in the off-season than baby-sit for their wives, apply themselves to the weight program at Coach Maylen's gym, or perhaps play basketball (at $100 a game) for the basketball team sponsored by the Chargers. The family men seem agreed that, because their wives are housebound all through the playing season, it is daddy's duty to ride herd on the young, so the girls may be turned loose during the off-season.

It is, if you forget the uneasiness that is basic to any job where injury or the loss of a bit of speed can chop a career short, a lazy life, particularly in this land, where the sun always shines. For the guys who are not given to trying to read their own stars, and who can keep themselves insulated from other men's woes, it is also a blissful life.

No matter what you may read, the playing of the game, regardless of hard hitting and bruises and danger of popped ligaments and cracked bones, is still fun as long as you stay healthy and strong and self-confident.

If there be flies in the ointment at all, they are the coaches who take pleasure in keeping a guy hanging on the edge, who will appraise a guy as "gone to hell" after one bad performance, and who will ride a guy endlessly for small mistakes. Or they are the few guys in the game who seem determined to rack an opponent up through cheap shots and late hitting. There are only a few of those. But they are the target of concentrated venom.

There is only one person alive whom John Hadl, for instance, really hates with all his soul. That is Ben Davidson of Oakland, the most notorious cheap-shot artist in the league. Studying in the game films his repeated efforts to spear a guy who is prostrate, to bang into a pile-up to earn some extra ink, the veterans will warn you again and again: "Watch out for that guy! Keep your eye on him! Don't relax if he's *anywhere* around!" Davidson seems to take most pleasure in grounding a quarterback with a late hit and it is efforts in this direction that have earned him John Hadl's loathing. Whenever John faces Davidson on the field, he applies to Ben, at the top of his lungs and without letting up, every dirty name the Lords of the Language ever took pains to keep out of print.

There are a number of guys who specialize in sliding into a pile-up, not with the intent of sneaking in a late blow but just so they may be seen getting up last from the sod and be given public credit for the effort. Davidson, through his efforts to get into every pile-up after the tackle has been made, actually gets credit for many tackles he had nothing to do with—just as Sam Huff used to. But Ben is also looking to zing anyone who is stupid enough to imagine that he is safe from injury just because he has let go of the ball or because the whistle has blown. When he goes late into a pile-up, he roars in, helmet first.

There are a few other guys who have reputations as cheap-shot artists, although there is none to match Davidson in the virulence of other players' dislike. Rickie Jack-

son, defensive end from Denver, is a man quarterbacks
are urged to keep an eye on at all times. And Ron
Pritchard, the Houston linebacker, is a noted head-hunter
—a guy who likes to deliver KO wallops with his taped
forearm, particularly when a quarterback is looking the
other way. I don't believe any quarterbacks are really
intimidated by these characters. Their presence on the
field just keeps you wary, for you know that any time the
official is looking the wrong way, you may get hit.

There is a tradition in pro football that men like this
eventually get caught up with, by design. But that is one
more tradition I am afraid that the modern game has
outgrown. Maybe everyone fears that a trade might land
him on the same club as one of these performers. Or
perhaps late-hitters and cheap-shot specialists, along with
speed-freaks, pot-heads, and guys who shoot babies in
Viet Nam, are all going to rate beatification in the New
Religion for Doing Their Own Thing.

Speaking of religion, that is not really so big a factor
in a football player's life as casual observation might
persuade you. Our club, like many other clubs, has a team
chaplain. Every Sunday, Father Murray holds services in
our motel, and most of the guys attend. Some few go to
their own church. But believe me, to most of the faithful
worshipers, attending that mass is like taking care to tie
your shoes in the same order and in the same fashion, or
not stepping on the sideline when you go on the field.
It is just going through a familiar routine to make sure
your luck doesn't desert you. Who wants to risk breaking
a leg by tempting the fairy godmother or the guardian
angel or the Great Spirit or the Fates? I have a feeling that
if Voodoo were fashionable in this country, the guys would
be just as ready to chant the proper phrases to keep
those gods temporarily appeased as they are to say their
prayers.

We do say a prayer before every game, when the club
kneels and hears the coach pray that nobody on *either* side
gets hurt. (Does Ben Davidson keep his fingers crossed in
his locker room? I wonder.) Then we all join in the
Lord's Prayer and I privately throw in a Hail Mary. But

all the while I note guys peeking up from beneath their brows to see if it is time to lift the head yet. So what we have is not really religion, it's ritual. And the guys subscribe to it with just as much fervor as they subscribe to the notion that it's bad news to break a mirror.

9

If I Were King . . . or Even Just a Coach

I was brought up to believe that people who find fault should be prepared to come up with alternatives, outlining how the world *should* be arranged. While I have no such program for the real world I do have one for the Dream World of pro football. It is not very complicated and not entirely original, but is derived from observation and conversation and unbridled self-confidence.

In general, I would like to see happen in pro football —in all football—what is happening in every organized activity in the land: a move toward control by the people who are employed or involved in it. As schools and universities yield up some authority over curriculum and discipline to the students, I would like to see pro football put its scheduling, its discipline, its training methods, and its divvy of the take more into the hands of the men who play the game and the guys who instruct them. More coaches ought to be general managers and part owners, so that owners who have no real knowledge of the game would not be able to mess with the strategy and so that coaches would have enough security not to have to waste time trying to find scapegoats or kissing rich men's asses. The players, through their organization, should have more control over scheduling, over signing and trading of players and over discipline, to create uniform playing conditions throughout the league, and to enforce minimum standards of personal freedom.

If I were coaching a club, I think the first thing I would do would be to update the bed-check system a little by recognizing the fact that most guys are bound to stay awake later. I would not insist on an early bedtime before a game, as long as the players were in the motel by midnight. In general, I think I would use a somewhat looser rein and try to suit the discipline to the individual (as the best coaches always do), tightening up on the guys who needed it and not riding so hard on the guys who knew how to pace themselves.

All the same, I believe I would stick to a system of fines for enforcing the rules. But I would make sure the fines, when they were imposed, were the same for everybody. On some clubs, a violation that costs some favorite $300, will cost a doghouse resident $1000. Unfair treatment of this sort is bad for team morale, for most of the guys will sympathize with the player who gets the rougher deal.

My training regime would be looser off the field and tighter on the field. I would try to eliminate the waste motions and the waste talk in practice, so that more plays could be run and *everybody* could leave with a feeling of accomplishment—and with the feeling too that he had been through a workout.

The day would start at noon, except for the guys who had injuries in need of care. The walking wounded would check into the treatment room in the morning. Everybody would be dressed and ready for meetings shortly before 1 P.M. The team meeting would last until 2 and everybody would be on the field at 2:30.

From then on, I would use about the same system as most clubs use, starting with random warm-up, then forty-yard sprints, then calisthenics, skeleton drills, and so on. The wind-up would be more "forties." But I would eliminate one drill that strikes me as a waste. In this the receivers run out to take passes while two defenders give them the bump-and-run treatment. This just throws everyone's timing off and does nothing to improve the performance of either passer or receiver. I would rely on a man's instincts to react to whatever sort of defensive treatment he came up against in a game.

The curfew on the Friday before a game would be 1

a.m. under my regime. And on Saturday night I would ask only that the guys be in their rooms by midnight. I would continue the practice of taking them all to an early movie, then turn them loose for a couple of hours.

As for pre-season work, I would rearrange that a little too. The rookies would report three weeks before the first pre-season game and the vets just two weeks before. Two-a-day drills would continue until the Wednesday before the first game, then the schedule would lighten.

During the two-a-day drills, I would have the guys in full pads in the morning and in shorts in the afternoon. For the first few days I would bear down on conditioning. And I would not at this time put too much emphasis on finesse. I am more for full effort in early practice than for fine execution. Nor would I go all-out to win the first few pre-season games. They would provide my chance to see my rookies in action, so that by the third game I'd have pruned the squad down to those I wanted to keep.

The guys who were turned loose would be protected (under the new deal I dream of) by a guaranteed minimum severance payment. And the "option clause" would be done away with, or put into a form that really gives the player a break. The current clause is a phony. It sets the man back a full year in his efforts to deal with another club. And it gives him no freedom anyway, for under the rules, Pete Rozelle, or whoever is commissioner, is permitted to designate what player or players must be handed over in payment to the original owner of the player's contract.

In practice this has usually meant that the team hiring the man had to give up *more* than his value. As a result, a man who is playing out his option has a hell of a time working out a deal. There being no other league (except Canada, where working conditions are not ideal) to supply any bargaining leverage, a player is just as tightly bound as he was before he decided to play the option out.

What is needed is some clause that will enable a man, within a certain period, and under certain restrictions, to make his own deal. The club needs some protection to enable it to maintain continuity as a team. But the player too needs some loosening of the bonds that have the power to keep him from ever realizing his true worth as a player.

As for the game itself, were I made all-powerful, I think I could sharpen that up, as a spectacle, and as a way of making a living. For one thing, I could try to make the officiating more consistent, not just by putting at least half the officials on full time but by the use of automatic oversight by means of cameras to make it possible to call certain violations, such as pass interference, correctly. I believe there is more controversy, and more discontent, over these calls than over anything else that goes wrong on the gridiron.

This is more true now than ever, for the new bump-and-run technique has created far more inconsistency in the calling of interference fouls. By the rules, if the "bump" is made after the ball is in the air, it is a violation. But the nearest official sometimes has his back turned to the quarterback and so cannot always tell when the ball has been thrown. So it has generally been the practice to allow a bump, when the defender is still in front of the receiver (at which point all the officials can see if the ball has been thrown) and to call a foul if he bumps the receiver after the receiver has gone by. But that has not always worked out, as we have had many occasions to note.

To solve this problem, I would deploy six cameras to cover the passer and all receivers and permit instant reruns on every reception. It would require only a few seconds, in response to an appeal, to determine finally and indisputably if there had been a violation. And it would incidentally be in accord with an ancient football tradition —the "referring" of foul-calls to the "referee." In the early versions of the game each team had an umpire (a "non-peer" or outsider) with his club's colors fastened to his cane. When he thought his boys had been mistreated, he would raise his cane and play would be halted while the referee would listen to both sides of the dispute and give his decision.

My system would give the referee an automatic observer no one could call partisan or unfair. It would remove a lot of the hysterical flak from the sidelines, hardly slow down the action at all (an incomplete pass kills the clock anyway), and make the whole game more enjoyable to the spectators and more satisfying to the players.

The offense has made efforts to cope with the bump-and-run and defensive holding by working to have fouls called every time. This would work well enough except for the fact that a quarterback can no more trust an official to call every foul than a batter can trust an umpire to call ball four on a pitch that misses the strike zone. Once or twice I have been successful in taking advantage of some obvious interference by getting the ball off in the direction of the foul. I did this once when I saw a safety man holding Willie Frazier. Immediately I let the ball go to Willie and the official quickly threw a flag.

Theoretically it should be possible to eliminate the illegal bump-and-run in the same manner, that is, by throwing the ball to the receiver you know is going to get bumped and throwing it quickly. But you will get a flag only if the official is properly positioned and happens to be looking. My camera system would make this a certainty, because it would catch the bump every time and also show the release of the ball.

There are a few other major changes that would increase the spectators' enjoyment too. Nowadays defense has come to dominate the game, so that a club with a mighty defense and a good place kicker can beat the best offense in the land. Indeed, when Hank Stram sounded off last year about his "Football of the Seventies" the players told each other that the true Football of the Seventies was not Hank's Power-I and moving pocket but "a strong defense and a Norwegian place kicker."

I think the offense could redress the balance a bit if the field were widened, as in Canada, so runners and receivers had more room to maneuver. I believe there would be more plays run if the clock were stopped on first down (as in college) until the markers had been set. Now officials sometimes have to hold up a play until the linesmen have caught up. I also believe the return of the two-point conversion would somewhat lessen the current dominance of the place-kicker.

The game is of course improving even without my ministrations. The specialty teams, which used to be just catchalls for the players who could not quite make it, now receive far more attention as coaches have come to realize that kick returns and kick coverage account for about one-third of the game.

The new I-formation has got the offensive moving and has helped open the game to a certain extent. Incidentally, Sid Gilman earned himself some extra respect from his players and indicated why he has been able to hold his own as a coach through many seasons when he openly changed his mind about this formation. Like many other coaches, Sid had at first belittled the Power-I as just another offensive formation and not an especially effective one. But in 1970 he announced frankly: "I was all wrong about the I-formation" and set out to make use of it.

One great advantage of the Power-I is the fact the ball carriers run straight paths to the holes instead of running slants. This shortens the distance to the opening, gives them a chance to slip more quickly through briefer holes, and makes the attack more explosive. The defense may choke off the offense at the point of attack but the runner, coming at right angles to the scrimmage line, can go either right or left, so that an extra two steps can give the runner wide options. In the old off-tackle slant, the runner had only two choices—turn inside the end or go around. Now the runner can go right or left, inside or outside.

The I is not a good pass formation, except on a first-down play-action pass. On third down and long yardage, the I simply does not allow the backs to deploy themselves swiftly enough to offer sufficient "underneath" coverage—"underneath" being the area inside the deep defensive backs.

The "big" play is being taken away from the offense nowadays as so many clubs have turned to zone defense. That is why I would like to see receivers given more room to operate. I also favor the use of multiple flankers—double and triple wing, or the use of three flankers on one side. The mobile quarterback and the "moving pocket" are both helping make the game more open, and there will be more efforts in this direction.

The game of pro football is spreading too. I do not believe it is anywhere near the saturation point. Before long I expect to see 32 teams in the league.

Some people say that more teams will mean more thinly spread talent and poorer play. I don't agree. Nowadays too many veterans are pushed out of the game because a coach does not want to miss out on a promising rookie. In this way great careers are cut short and some men never attain the heights they might have reached if there had been a few more years left to them. Quarterbacks especially will often have their very best years only as they draw close to their forties, for, if they manage to stay in good physical shape, they will then have more craft, more resourcefulness, more adaptability, and will own more of the respect and confidence of their teammates.

Billy Cannon was a guy who was forced to retire too soon. He could not have been over 34 when he quit and he had at least two more good years. There are others who never starred as Cannon did. Not too many runners are as durable as Billy Cannon but most of them should be good for seven or eight seasons at least. Wide receivers should not fade before they are in their late thirties and linemen should last a bit longer. Keeping veterans in action longer will mean better football, not worse. It will make for more security and more fan interest.

If I had charge of such matters, I would issue a ruling that all football stadiums had to be big enough to hold 70,000 spectators. Before another decade is out, there would not be a seat to spare in any of them. But along with the added capacity would go a new deal of some sort for the players, so that they could cut a larger slice of the increased income. Someone should be appointed to throw a flag when the club owners are caught screwing the uniformed employees.

But pro football is not the only aspect of the game that would get my attention were I to be granted the dictatorial power I sometimes yearn for. I would move for the creation of a National Commission to protect the college player too, so that the men who are recruited for college in order to play football would get what the contract really implies—a university education—or get a living wage plus job security.

I suppose the ideal way to arrange a course of studies for the young men who are playing football to earn their way through college would be to permit them to give their full time to football from the first day of practice until the end of the playing season. They would, for that period each year, study no subject except the one from which they most likely hope to earn their immediate livelihood—the subject being football. Then, during the rest of the year, including a summer semester, they could concentrate on academic subjects.

Short of a scheme like that, I believe football "majors" should be allowed to take whatever subjects they are qualified to assimilate. Now, in the Phys Ed universities, football "scholars" are too often forbidden to take subjects that will eat too deeply into their concentration. As a result, we have the spectacle of college graduates who can neither speak grammatical English nor grasp the subtleties of a Ronald Reagan campaign speech.

In the football schools, a serious injury often means the end of education—either in football or in Greek. While most such schools stop short of simply expelling an athlete for having the bad taste to break a bone or rip a muscle apart in practice, many of them will insist that the injured man show up every day for the workout, and will thus force him to quit school in self-defense. A National Commission to require fair play for college athletes would prevent such abuses and would also allow such men to pursue whatever studies they had time and taste for. Now the universities more or less regulate themselves on such matters and do it about as heartily as the automobile industry enforces its own safety standards.

I am not arguing for an end to college football or to the recruited athlete, or even for a limit on the study of physical education and its related disciplines, but just for an end to hypocrisy in this one area of our lives. What a guy learns when he works out the terms of a football scholarship at one of the standard factories is that horse-shit is the major (and approved) constituent in all formal discourse—that no one with good sense really believes what newspapers print, or college presidents propose, or government leaders propound, and that the *authentic* word is what is offered out of the side of the mouth when regular guys meet in private conclave.

The old-time Spartan atmosphere is already disappearing from college athletic squads, even in the schools where football and basketball are almost the only subjects taught with a whole heart. Just ten years ago athletes were con-fined to dorms like gladiators and had to have the type of haircut the coach approved, or else go home. They were, it is true, offered first-rate medical care in most major colleges, although there was still a tradition that too much concern over an injury was somehow effeminate and that it was better to have a "trainer" pull you together with adhesive tape than be taken to a hospital. The medical care is still good. But nowadays college kids are more aware of their rights and will not stand still for the sort of regimentation that was supposed to "make a man" out of you by forcing you to obey orders like a pack animal. And in today's colleges it is no longer considered sissified to ask that a medical doctor and not a retired wrestler check over your injuries.

Pro football has suffered some in the public mind, I think, because it still bears the horseshit odor that sur-rounds the game in some of the big universities. But as the pro game has become the big game in the country, that aroma has faded and instead its fans, and especially its young fans, have begun to recognize that football is one profession where a guy really makes it on his brains and ability and courage.

Women are supposd to be the natural enemies of foot-ball because it devours so many TV hours that might be devoted to matters of the mind, such as "Hee-Haw" and "Peyton Place." But in my life I have not found this to be so. Girls make up a large and informed share of the football audience. There are many I know who can decipher a football formation as adeptly as a man, and far more knowledgeably than some sportswriters I have met. Indeed, I never could see why girls could not cover all sports, including football, or why press boxes and press rooms should be run on a stag basis. The presence of girls in those retreats might cut down some on the drinking, and perhaps rid them of the high-school-fraternity air that encourages juvenility. As I said in the beginning, I just cannot imagine football without girls and I think their importance to the game should be acknowledged.

I do not agree that there is any immediate danger that football will die of overexposure. On the contrary, I think that as it expands and as it becomes a better game (with some alterations to give the offense back its original importance) there will hardly be a stadium in the land that is not sold out. The games that people play to try to inject meaning into their lives are none of them as exciting or as on-the-level as pro football is. The major games—war, and business, and, God forgive me, even organized religion—have all begun to pall on their participants so fast that only massive applications of drugs (including, of course, alcohol) can keep them bearable. Ultimately, I think, when people can manage to turn their minds from the serious concerns of the race—feeding the hungry, sheltering the destitute, comforting the forlorn, and promoting the world-wide general welfare—they will give them frankly to true recreations and not to games that try to pretend they are the chief concern of man.

I find young people today smarter and more aware and less likely to be deluded by the myths our fathers lived by. And I know that young people are also more sympathetic fans, more inclined to favor the players, to understand how easy it is to make a mistake, to comprehend the learning process, and to enjoy the contest without bitterly disowning the losers. Of course the instinctive urge to win will remain the chief incentive of football as it is in all competitive games. But fans who are more secure in their own lives are less likely to need to work off their own frustrations on the hapless "goat" of a football disaster.

This look into the future is also a look right into the present. It is not tomorrow but now that young people will demand more voice in their own destiny. Football scholarship students will ask for, and should receive, the right to pursue even a medical career if they choose (or even stick frankly and openly to athletics). The young people who enter college on academic scholarships today are no longer required (and would not allow themselves to be required) to submit to a rigid program of study. When my new Central Committee for College Athletes comes into being (financed by the colleges out of the athletic budget but appointed by the federal government and including student representatives) it will cover all varsity sports and will guarantee to every subsidized athlete the right to select a course of study suited to his aims as well as his abilities. As long as he (or she) produces on the field (or is prevented by occupational injury from performing) he should own that right to a complete education.

I don't believe it is going to require a revolution or even my installation as dictator to accomplish this. Colleges are going to continue to recruit athletes heavily as long as people will pay money to watch games. But today's athletes are more worldly wise (or street-smart), are more at home under public pressure, and are not going to be so easy to take advantage of as were the country boys of our daddy's age.

10

The Domres All-Stars

The best active quarterback in the league right now (and this is John Hadl's choice too) is Joe Namath. Bad knees and all, Joe is still the champ. He throws better, reacts faster, and thinks more quickly than any of his rivals. Unfortunately, a quarterback, under present conditions, cannot by himself drag his team into the Superbowl. Without a sturdy defense, a quarterback can complete 30 passes a game and still come in second.

But with a tough defense to take the ball away from the enemy, Joe is the man I would count on to win the big games. The view I had of him in the 1969 Superbowl was enough to convince me that Joe had no equal. Undoubtedly Johnny Unitas and Bart Starr and Y. A. Tittle have been great ones but Tittle is gone and Johnny and Bart are fading. None of them now can match Joe in picking a defense apart, in anticipating defensive moves, and in quickness of release, i.e., getting the ball off in a hurry. Joe seems to have the ball in the air the very instant his eye lights on an open receiver and when he is getting the protection he deserves he is matchless in getting the ball on target. Weeb Ewbank's method of having the defensive line meet the charge at the line of scrimmage, instead of dropping off to adjust to the stunts, gives Joe an opportunity to set up without always dropping back as far as other quarterbacks need to.

Joe is also a thoroughly decent citizen—friendly, unassuming, and relaxed. He often visits John at his home in San Diego, where he enjoys getting out of the spotlight, playing with the kids, and idly rapping. Joe has been marked conceited by some observers but John, who knows him intimately, has never seen any evidence of excessive self-esteem in Joe. Nor have I. He is as mild-mannered and easy-going a man as you would ever want to have with you.

My first choice of fullbacks would be Ron Johnson of the New York Giants. He is not the fastest runner alive by any means but he is damn fast. And he can run over tacklers, or he can elude them because of his remarkable skill at changing direction in mid-stride. Johnson is the one man we were all impressed with as we watched the game films of the Giants. And when we saw him put in the flanker's spot as his team reached the 12-yard line in one game, we knew that the Giants' brass shared our opinion of his versatility. Fullback to flanker—there can be no greater flattery than that for a coach to hand a ball carrier. Johnson in that game justified his club's confidence by running a short post pattern from the flanker position and grabbing the ball for a touchdown.

Our own Dickie Post would be my choice for a running back. Dickie cannot match some of the great sprinters in speed but he is as shifty as a spider. He is too small to bowl over any defensive men but he can jive-step his way out of difficulties better than anyone I ever saw and will dodge all over the field to avoid contact. His coolness in combat I have already described as well as his willingness to go back for more. The easiest play in the book, for the quarterback, is the quick hand-off that leads to the 80-yard run for a touchdown. And the man I would most like to hand off to on that play is Dickie. Brad Hubbert is the man to bowl over a defender to get that extra yard. Dickie is the guy to break away and keep going forever.

I saw Dickie at his utmost in my rookie year in the game against the Jets. We were deep in our own territory, inside the two-yard line I think, and John Hadl was struggling for a little elbow room. In hopes of getting an extra three or four yards, John called Dickie on an off-tackle play. Dickie darted for the hole and found no hole there. Not being a man to bang through a defense, Dickie bounced off and went outside. The corner back charged up to make the tackle and Dickie gave him about four moves, then left the guy flatfooted. Dickie cut back then against the defensive flow, ducked past the strong safety, who just got a finger on him, and then jived and weaved and sprinted away for some 40 yards before they finally caught him. All alone, he turned the situation right around.

No one would want better receivers on his side than Lance Alworth and Gary Garrison, whose skills I have already described at length. Despite Lance's penchant for creating his own patterns without warning, he is the greatest at saving a quarterback from an incompletion by his leaps and flips, his ability to reverse himself, and his skill at hanging on to passes that just about scrape his fingernails. When a pass is underthrown and both Lance and the defender go up for it, it is almost a dead certainty that Lance will be the one to bring it down. He can leap like a fish and hold any ball he can put a hand on. I am sorry I won't be throwing to him this season.

Gary is equally adept at holding tight to a ball once he gets flesh on it. For the past two years he has led the league in touchdown receptions and seems likely to lead it for several more, because he is one of the most spectacular open-field runners in the game. I still have a picture in my mind of our pre-season game with the Rams in my rookie year when Gary took a short quick-out from John Hadl at the Ram 40 and dodged all over the field. He threw three fakes at Clancy Williams and left Clancy gaping and empty-handed. Eddie Meador took a desperation dive at Gary at the final moment and managed to get a hand on him but Gary never lost his balance and ripped in for the score.

I have to say, however, that, were Gary not available, I'd go for Fred Biletnikoff, Oakland's wide receiver, who can also pluck a ball off his fingertips and carry it a long way. I think the greatest play I ever saw Biletnikoff make came in a game against us. Oakland had the ball about on our 30, driving in. Biletnikoff ran a corner pattern and the pass led him so far that had he dived for it he'd have landed out of bounds. So he sprinted top speed, reached out one hand, and almost at the instant the ball touched his fingers, he glanced down at the sideline. He clutched the ball in one hand, tapped *both* feet in-bounds, and plunged over the line with the ball snuggled to his chest. *Everybody* had to cheer that touchdown.

Tight ends generally, like fullbacks, have to be guys able to run the medium patterns that put them right in there among the linebackers who can reach out an arm and almost remove a guy's head from his shoulders. So they are mostly men physical enough to bowl over linemen and linebackers and still use their speed to get loose. The flankers prefer to stick to the perimeter, where those big hairy arms don't reach out and belt you across the neck. But Charlie Sanders of Detroit, my first choice, can make a linebacker think twice about standing up to him. Charlie also has, in addition to his strength and size, really extraordinary speed and agility, so that he can sprint away like a flanker and is acrobatic enough to turn out-of-bounds passes into touchdowns in the Biletnikoff manner.

In fact, Charlie did just that in a Thanksgiving Day game against Oakland in 1970, when Detroit had the ball on the Oakland 12-yard line. Landry called a pass to Sanders on a corner pattern but Charlie was well covered by Atkinson on the play and Landry had to lob the ball over Atkinson's head. Actually the ball went out of bounds and there was no way Charlie could get his hands on it except by projecting himself through the air head first in a desperation dive. He flung himself headlong, grabbed hold of the ball beyond the sideline, then, in a remarkable demonstration of agility, managed to tap both toes on the ground before his body struck. His toes dragged clearly across the chalk as he fell, so it was a touchdown, even though, when Charlie brought the ball down, he was the full length of his body out of bounds. That is the kind of fast-thinking, fast-acting, and agile guy I'd be happy to throw passes to.

I have not been around enough really, nor paid close enough attention, to size up offensive linemen in the league. I do not play opposite them and am not given to studying their moves, so I have no favorites. I do know, however, that offensive linemen, from the right end over to the opposite tackle, have got to be men who like to *hit* and men who are big enough and strong enough to make their hitting count. A man who is given to imagining what the blow may feel like, or wondering if there will be an injury, or anticipating a harder blow in return, will not be fast enough in his movements to succeed in this job. An offensive lineman has got to get off the mark a split second before the ball. (If the ball is to be snapped on "hut-two," for instance, he will charge on the "t" sound of "hut.") If he wastes that split second cringing inwardly from the result of his charge, he is going to get beaten.

Smart, experienced linemen can eliminate a lot of direct hitting, in which they may be at a disadvantage because of a wide weight differential, by using "position blocking" —by maintaining a certain position in relation to the other guy's body until the play goes by. Or they may simply "ride" the guy past the play by keeping him trying to get around them. This is a matter of beating the opponent to the punch and making contact in a position from which he cannot merely throw you off. It is at the goal line, however, that the all-pros reveal their special talents. Here the struggle is strictly physical and no finesse is possible. It is up to the offensive lineman simply to blast into the enemy and neutralize him until the ball carrier takes the ball over.

Incidentally, in these moments of crisis in a game— when a big play is needed, or an extra yard required to stay in the game, to keep a drive going, to make a score —even the quarterback must be prepared to turn "physical" and be ready to *go*, instead of ducking for the sideline or sliding to the ground. Joe Namath has it in him to maintain a club's momentum this way, to carry the ball right into a defender, in the Joe Kapp manner, to get the extra foot or two. When a quarterback makes a play like that, and especially if he takes a hard tackle or a late hit, he can get a team suddenly psyched up and ready to rip into the foe.

You'll hear the change of spirit in the huddle as the

guys tell each other: "Come on! We've got it now! We've got it!"

Of course some guys just can't succeed in bowling over a defensive man. New York's Fran Tarkenton, for instance, will never punish a defender no matter how he tries. But Gabriel and Kapp continually excite their mates by belting a defensive man into a spin, for those guys can bull right through a tackle.

On defense you have to judge the lines as units—the "front four" that is dedicated to making a quarterback's days unhappy and his nights full of pain. To me it is almost impossible to choose between the front defensive units of the 1970 Vikings and the 1970 Rams. Perhaps, from knowing them at first hand, I'll have to give the edge to the Rams—and particularly to Olsen and Jones, two men who attack with the ferocity of mad bulls and the reactions of wildcats. Of all the guys I would rather not see charging at me as I set up to pass, the four front men of the 1970 Rams are the ugliest and best.

In my defensive backfield I would most like to have a few of the guys from the Kansas City Chiefs. As a matter of fact, and in the face of all contrary publicity, I will rate Willie Lanier of Kansas City ahead of Dick Butkus of Chicago. Willie does not even get the publicity that Atlanta's Tommy Nobis gets and Willie is better than Nobis. Willie and Butkus are the two best in the business at linebacker. Both hit exceptionally hard. Both have lots of knowledge and react instinctively to every sort of offense. Both will really punish a ball carrier. But Willie is faster than Dick and Willie's range is phenomenal.

And then there is Bobby Bell of Kansas City, who is like lightning in the power with which he strikes and the speed with which he reacts. I have good reason to remember Bobby because he pulled a defensive play on me that is supposed to be impossible: He covered *two* men on a pass play—the primary receiver and the secondary receiver.

I had called a sideline slant to Lance because the Kansas City zone defense usually rotates toward the field. On this play, one back goes straight out into the flat from the line of scrimmage, while Lance goes four yards deep and then slants at a 45-degree angle for the post. This is supposed to put the linebacker in a bind, because he has to cover one man or the other and cannot cover both.

But Bobby, reading my eyes, promptly took the slant away from Lance. I turned immediately and let fly to the man in the flat. But Bobby had anticipated my reaction and had hurled his body toward the path of the ball just as I let fly. He reached the damn ball too, knocked it down with one hand, and came within a hair of holding on to it for an interception. I don't think there was anybody on the field or in the stands who appreciated the brilliance of Bobby's maneuver as I did. Bobby acted as if he did that every day. He was sore at himself for not holding on to the ball.

K. C.'s Johnny Robinson has to be in my defensive backfield too, if only for the work he did in the Superbowl against the Vikings. Playing with a couple of cracked ribs that just had to hurt, Johnny intercepted three Minnesota passes. Johnny is probably the most reliable defender in the league. When he's needed, he's there. He is one of the great players who, along with that "Norwegian place kicker," keep the Chiefs in contention even when their "Offense of the Seventies" is sputtering like an offense from 1942.

But not all the great defensive backs play in Kansas City. Detroit has a real genius in Lem Barney, who can join my club whenever he wants. Lem can carry the ball better than many a halfback and he reacts to trouble like a cat, fighting to maintain his marvelous balance and looking for new ways to hurt the enemy. Once I saw him, in fielding a punt, slam hard against his goal post, with force enough to lay an ordinary man low. But Lem spun away, wobbling, floundered for just a second or two to get his feet under him, and then took off upfield, faking, dodging, weaving, jiving for 50 yards before they brought him down.

And we have one of the best in Pete Barnes, who is a born athlete, with the flowing movement, the grace, the balance, the speed, and the fiery confidence that mark a man an athlete even when he is just flipping a ball around on a basketball court. Pete differs from all others of his kind in that he has no fear at all of being isolated against a running back. He just loves such a challenge and has yet to find the man he cannot stay up with. When he tackles a ball carrier he keeps his face up, seeming to look right through his target so that he can see himself going clear to the other side. He does actually explode *through* a runner, not satisfied merely to hold him or stop him but bent on slicing him down. What he seems to like best is closing on the receiver of a screen pass. He smells out such a play almost instinctively and zeroes in on the receiver so swiftly that no one can hold him off. The home crowd always roars its satisfaction on seeing Pete nail a man on a screen and put him into the air. No one breaks through Pete's tackles, or bounces off. It is the lucky ones who land rightside up.

11

What Now?

Right this minute what I want most in all the world, for myself, is a chance to play football. And I don't want to find myself secretly hoping, in spite of my better self, that my best friend, John Hadl, suffers another serious injury. No quarterback can ride the bench for weeks and still keep his skills sharp. For one thing, the reserve quarterback finds himself shut out from passing practice even in drills. Inasmuch as Hadl, naturally, has to get the work in during the skeleton drills, I doubt if I throw more than a couple of dozen passes all week. I look forward to games now because I get more chance to throw before the game begins than I get any other time.

Inability to keep your eye sharp in practice is bound to affect your play in a game, so that when you do get in, you have to waste time just getting yourself back in the groove. And sometimes you can throw the game away in the process. Also your reactions are somewhat slower. You lose those instinctive moves that you make without thinking and that often can keep you from getting sacked or can help you bang over a tackler.

I have worked out with the heavy weights for a long time and have put a lot of extra power into my arm, so that I can throw farther and faster. My next plan is to get my weight down to increase my stamina and speed. I hope to weigh in for the current season at about 205 (now I'm just under 220). But I have got to *play*.

Naturally I know that there must be something in my life besides football. Why else would I chew my ass out this way? I mean to find time to study too so that when my 20-year career is done and I am carried off the field on the shoulders of my weeping admirers, I will be qualified to do something that will leave the world somehow better off for my having been here. In my more peaceful moments I contemplate moving to New Zealand, a land where life moves more slowly, where people have a chance to know each other and there is (so it is said) no scramble to lay your hands on somebody's unwatched nickels. I have read and talked much about that land. It seems to be now about in the state New England was in more than half a century ago, when a man could still support himself and his family from the soil. Would they need lawyers there? It doesn't matter because I could turn to farming as readily as to law (or football) and perhaps be even better at it. And I am getting better and better at football.

Place-kicking has become so important in football (a team without a strong offense is completely lost without a good place-kicker) that I wish I could take some practice in that. I have played a lot of rugby, have always kicked well, and my leg is good enough to get proper distance. But the coaches have promised me that it will cost me $100 every time they see me kicking. And I don't blame them. It *is* possible to pull a muscle just kicking the ball and a pulled muscle would ground me for weeks.

But I want to play.

At the same time, I have no yen to be traded. I want to play for the Chargers and I want to play for Sid Gilman, who is one of the few coaches who can actually *teach* men playing techniques, and who is usually one jump ahead of the enemy in strategy. So I suppose what I am hoping for is a chance to divide the job with John so that when, after four or five more good seasons and a trip to the Superbowl, John goes into retirement, I will know the job as well as he does.

My style of playing is strictly mine. I am not a Joe Kapp type, with a yen to charge recklessly downfield holding the ball in my arms. I hope for good solid pass protection that will enable me to do the sort of job I enjoy—trying to anticipate and out-think the opposition and only occasionally, when the other guy least expects it, putting the ball on my hip and taking off around end on my own. I think I am passing better now than ever. I'll miss Lance, but there are still good receivers on our club. My confidence keeps on growing, even in idleness, and I took forward to the first game as a kid looks forward to Christmas.

I have read most of what some of the discontented ex-players have said about the sorry aspects of the pro game. On some counts I am sure they are right. But there is no such burgeoning traffic in drugs as Dave Meggyesey, for instance, hints, nor is there likely to be. The alleged brutalities of the game are partly in the mind. The game is *rough*. So is baseball. So is professional basketball. So is hockey. There are many men in the world who like to play rough games, they being big enough and strong enough to exchange punishment with their equals and to glory in it.

I am sure Dave Meggyesey was that way himself for a long time, or he would not have stayed so long in the game. Frankly, I just don't believe his tale of a sort of involuntary servitude all his life. I *know* he must have enjoyed the game the way so many of us do. I am convinced that his "enlightenment," or whatever it was, was a latter-day revelation that may have had as much to do with his life outside of football as it did with what happened on and around the gridiron. I know that if I did not honestly enjoy the game, actually relish the contact and the sense of accomplishment you can derive from it, I would have quit long ago. Instead, as I said at the beginning, if I could not get paid for playing, I would still play. Perhaps I'd turn to rugby, which is fast and rough and exciting and in some ways more demanding than American football. But I would sure as hell be out with a gang of big guys somewhere, when I could, throwing and kicking and running with the football.

Most pro players enjoy the game too, despite the griping they may go in for during two-a-day practice sessions and when they are disciplined by the coach. Nearly every player is motivated by his own pride to give an extreme effort when victory is within reach. And the chance of attaining the top prize and the top money will make men struggle to get back into the play even when their bones complain.

I just hope that the pro game does not turn completely money-oriented and that the scheduling of extra games is less reckless, that more concern is given to the welfare of the players and to the opportunity of the ordinary fan, especially the young fan, to watch the game. There seems to be a slight movement now in the direction that baseball followed, and that has helped put that game in second place—not so much from over-exposure as from too much concern with maximizing profits, boosting ticket prices, shifting franchises, working in additional games, catering to the friends and associates of the club owners, as well as to the sportswriters—as if *they* were the guys who brought the customers in.

Players' salaries should go up and some way should be evolved to give the players more security. No one with any sense wants to standardize wages or keep men from bargaining individually for all they can get. But the journeyman player should be able to have a better sense of belonging and a better chance to get his share of the millions his efforts are earning for others.

The Monday night games should be limited, so that players do not get stuck with more than one a season. The loss of that extra day of rest can seriously cut into a player's stamina if it is repeated too often. It may be of course that more games could be played if rosters were bigger. But somehow I have the feeling that coaches would still go with their best every game—and fans would not want to feel that they were watching the B squads in action.

No doubt there is plenty of gambling on pro football. But gambling has never been a problem among the Chargers and I doubt if it ever will become one again in the professional game. Players are leery of risking their careers and most of them are possessed of a competitive spirit that would never permit them to play less than their best.

Pro football has been good to a great many people, to me among others. Where else would a guy like me find a chance to achieve early independence, to the point where he has time to fret over what contribution he can make to the world when his "career" is over? I think pro football, along with baseball and basketball, has helped to stifle a lot of race prejudice, has taught bigots to hold their tongues, and has helped raise a generation of young sport fans to whom racial discrimination is actually repellent.

No doubt throughout pro football there are Cradle Confederates who still harbor prejudice against men who were born black. Black players, because their opportunities for earning high salaries outside of sports remain limited, often find temselves at a disadvantage in salary negotiations. But that is not a situation peculiar to pro football.

The major ailments of the game are the ailments of the world outside— the "Fuck you, Jack! I'm all right!" philosophy that pervades the business and political world and that keeps men scurrying to grab off a few extra bucks and conniving to screw each other. In pro football I guess that shows up most often in recruiting which, in the past, has been reasonably uncivilized, with whole squads of "scouts" assigned to baby-sitting with athletes, to fend off emissaries from the rival league, and to use bribes and undercover arrangements as standard operating procedure.

Now the leagues have been merged into one and recruiting is organized and carefully supervised. But I can't help observing that many of the guys who used to slip fees to college coaches, scheme out ways to tie up college prospects before graduation, assign baby-sitters, round up the booze and the broads meant to keep college prospects from letting their attention wander, and okay the verbal "understandings" that were used to circumvent the rule against signing prospects before the college season was over—that these guys are still active in the game. Well, perhaps our Commissioner can keep them all in hand now, or at least keep them where he can watch them.

I don't want to see pro football become so thoroughly commercialized that rich men and their sons will be running the clubs from front offices. I prefer the guys who have taken up the game as a hobby and look on the profits as just a thin icing on a very luscious cake, who don't give

themselves any airs as football strategists, who have faith
in their coaches, allow them to run the show, and let them
share in the success, and who are more delighted to have
the Superbowl Trophy in the office than an overflowing
balance sheet.

It's not my fault that so many of the men who play
and coach football and operate the teams, and even a good
percentage of those who follow the game are people who
would rate as "squares" in any league. I allow people to
be different from me and I ask only that they grant me
the same privilege. I am not going to subscribe to their
doctrine that "winning is the *only* thing." And they don't
need to espouse any tenets of mine. I agree that the only
way to enjoy a competitive game is to play it to win, that
the "character-building" aspects of sport are largely for
losers, and that competitive sports, particularly contact
sports, satisfy something elemental in man's nature that
no amount of mechanization will ever breed out of him.

But I am damned if I see the need to pretend that football is an end in itself. And I am especially revolted by
those chest-beaters and drum-beaters who try to present
war as if it were just another great sport like football to be
enjoyed and "played" blindly, who pretend there is something especially manly about going out to kill other people
without bothering to question the purpose, and who parrot
that sterile nonsense about their being "no substitute for
victory!" It strikes me that many millions of the world's
people have had to discover substitutes for victory.

I have many such far-out theories of my own. I like to
wear my hair long and may even some day decide to sport
a beard. I don't believe that we have any God-given right
to spend Asian lives to save American lives. I am in favor
of girls—in the press box as well as in the cocktail lounge.
I think sportswriters should be given courses in the sports
they are trying to write about. I think the two-point conversion should return to football. I believe there should
be a "no-harm, no-foul" rule on holding and pass interference, so flags would not be thrown for violations that
could not possibly have affected the play.

And while I am baring my soul, let me confess to a

deed I was guilty of last season. One day, when the coaches came in to a meeting, they found chalked in large letters on the blackboard: "Spiro Agnew is Rosemary's Baby." They went into a froth of indignation and decided finally that a blasphemy like that could only have been put there by one of those "kookie long-haired Communists" that sometimes worked the projector.

Well, it wasn't a kookie long-haired projectionist at all. It was a kookie long-haired quarterback—namely, me.

SAN DIEGO CHARGERS
1970 ROSTER

SAN DIEGO CHARGERS—1970

No.	Name	Pos.	Ht.	Wt.	Age	Year	College
14	DOMRES, Marty	QB	6-4	215	23	2	Columbia
15	MERCER, Mike	K	6-0	215	34	10	Northern Arizona
18	CLARK, Wayne	QB	6-2	200	23	R	U.S. International
19	ALWORTH, Lance	WR	6-0	180	30	9	Arkansas
21	HADL, John	QB	6-1	218	30	9	Kansas
22	POST, Dickie	RB	5-9	190	24	4	Houston
24	HOWARD, Bob	CB	6-1	190	26	4	San Diego St.
25	GARRETT, Mike	RB	5-9	200	26	5	USC
26	HUBBERT, Brad	RB	6-1	240	29	4	Arizona
27	GARRISON, Gary	WR	6-1	193	26	5	San Diego St.
29	PARTEE, Dennis	K	6-1	218	24	3	SMU
35	DETWILER, Chuck	S	6-0	185	22	R	Utah State
37	FOSTER, Gene	RB	6-0	220	28	6	Arizona St.
39	HILL, Jim	S	6-2	190	24	2	Texas A&I
40	BEAUCHAMP, Joe	CB	6-0	185	26	5	Iowa State
42	SMITH, Dave	RB	6-1	210	22	R	Utah
43	TOLBERT, Jim	S	6-3	207	26	5	Lincoln
44	FLETCHER, Chris	CB	5-11	185	21	R	Temple
47	QUEEN, Jeff	RB	6-1	220	24	2	Morgan St.
50	PROTZ, Jack	LB	6-1	218	24	R	Syracuse
51	LENKAITIS, Bill	G	6-4	265	24	3	Penn St.
56	BRUGGERS, Bob	LB	6-1	224	26	5	Minnesota
59	BARNES, Pete	LB	6-1	247	25	4	Southern U.
60	BABICH, Bob	LB	6-2	230	23	R	Miami (O)
65	GRUNEISEN, Sam	C	6-1	250	29	9	Villanova
66	REDMAN, Rick	LB	6-0	230	27	6	Washington
69	GORDON, Ira	G	6-3	268	21	R	Kansas St.
70	WASHINGTON, Russ	T	6-6	295	24	3	Missouri
72	OWENS, Joe	DE	6-2	235	23	R	Alcorn A&M
75	FERGUSON, Gene	DT	6-8	300	22	2	Norfolk St.
76	OWENS, Terry	T	6-7	275	26	5	Jacksonville St.
78	SWEENEY, Walt	G	6-4	256	29	8	Syracuse
79	RICE, Andy	DT	6-2	268	28	5	Texas Southern
81	STAGGS, Jeff	DE	6-2	246	26	4	San Diego St.
82	DeLONG, Steve	DT	6-2	252	27	6	Tennessee
83	FRAZIER, Willie	TE	6-4	250	28	7	Arkansas AM&N
84	GILLETTE, Walker	WR	6-5	198	23	R	Richmond
86	BILLINGSLEY, Ron	DT	6-8	290	25	4	Wyoming
87	WILLIAMS, Tom	DE	6-4	250	22	R	Cal-Davis
89	STROZIER, Art	TE	6-2	220	24	R	Kansas St.

CHARGERS FUTURE LIST

No.	Name	Pos.	Ht.	Wt.	Age	Year	College
*20	SMITH, Russ	RB	6-0	212	26	4	Miami
45	DUNCAN, Leslie	S	5-10	175	28	7	Jackson State
49	EBER, Rick	WR	6-0	185	25	3	Tulsa
55	PORTER, Jack	C	6-3	240	22	R	Oklahoma
57	WITHROW, Cal	C	6-3	245	22	R	Kentucky
58	JONES, Harris	G	6-4	233	24	R	Johnson C. Smith
*64	SCHMEDDING, Jim	G	6-2	250	24	3	Weber State

*Injured Reserve

Head Coach: Charlie Waller
Assistants: Joe Madro, Red Cochran, Hal Herring, Bum Phillips,
Jackie Simpson, Jim Phillips

Hey There Sports Fan!

We have something just for *you!*

Bestselling paperbacks by and about the greatest pro's in the world of sports. Pro's like Tony Jacklin, Jerry Kramer, Bill Bradley and Arthur Ashe. So start building your own personal library right away. Ask for any of these books at your local bookstore, or use the handy coupon below. Find out what really makes a superstar run!